THE HERMIT SHELL

**Other Cambridge Reading books
you may enjoy**

Spindle River
Judith O'Neill

Heroes and Villains
Edited by Tony Bradman

Twinkle, Twinkle, Planet Blue
Poems selected by Morag Styles

**Other books by Frances Usher
you may enjoy**

That Rebellious Towne

Face to Face

Tell Alice

The Waiting Game

The Hermit Shell

Frances Usher

Illustrated by Liz Minichiello

CAMBRIDGE
UNIVERSITY PRESS

Cambridge Reading

General Editors
Richard Brown and Kate Ruttle

Consultant Editor
Jean Glasberg

PUBLISHED BY THE PRESS SYNDICATE OF THE UNIVERSITY OF CAMBRIDGE
The Pitt Building, Trumpington Street, Cambridge CB2 1RP, United Kingdom

CAMBRIDGE UNIVERSITY PRESS
The Edinburgh Building, Cambridge CB2 2RU, United Kingdom
40 West 20th Street, New York, NY 10011-4211, USA
10 Stamford Road, Oakleigh, Melbourne 3166, Australia

First published 1998

Printed in the United Kingdom at the University Press, Cambridge

Typeset in Concorde

A catalogue record for this book is available from the British Library

ISBN 0 521 55666 X   paperback

*This book is dedicated with
great respect to the men and women
of the Lifeboat Service.*

Contents

"The largest British Hermit Crab is *Pagurus bernhardus*, Common Hermit Crab, that occurs all round the British Isles. Small specimens are frequently found scrambling around in pools on the mid and lower shore. They always have their soft and vulnerable abdomens safely tucked into empty shells . . . Each shell is usually explored carefully both inside and out before the Hermit finally chooses one to its liking and the changeover from the old to the new shell is quite rapid as during the process the animal is vulnerable . . . When the hermit retreats into the shell the larger of its two claws (usually the right) can conveniently block the entrance . . ."

A Guide to the Seashore by Ray Ingle (Hamlyn 1969)

CHAPTER ONE

The Crab on the Fax

Neil Loftus lived in a Rest Home. It wasn't very restful, though, especially first thing in the morning.

On that Friday morning when the fax arrived, his mother came to wake him up. She pulled back his curtains and let in the thin January dawn.

"Looks like being a nice day," she said.

Neil opened his eyes and shut them again. He thought, it doesn't. It looks like being an awful day. Just like yesterday. Just like every day lately.

Down the passage the phone was ringing and ringing. "Who's that ringing?" he asked. "Is it Dad?"

"Probably," said Mum, going out again. "It usually is. Now, don't go back to sleep."

He heard her footsteps going on down the passage and the sound of her tapping on the door of Room 2.

"Time to get up, Winnie dear," she called. She always spoke to the residents very clearly, because they were all elderly and some of them were rather deaf. "Looks like being a nice day."

Neil lay still, thinking about the day ahead, thinking about another day of trying to keep away from Martyn and Lee.

The phone was still ringing. Why couldn't Mum answer it? Neil knew why. It was because Dad was calling.

Wearily, he rolled out of bed and padded down the passage. The phone hung on the wall at the far end, outside Room 6. Mum was in Room 3 now, talking to Mr Parsons. He was ninety-five and had only moved in last week. He was still a bit confused by the getting-up routine.

Br-Brr. Br-Brr.

Just before Neil reached the phone, the door of Room 6 flew open. He called out, "It's all right, Miss Cobham, I'm getting it," but he was too late.

"Dratted thing." Miss Cobham snatched up the phone. "Right outside my room, nobody ever bothering to answer . . . Hello. This is Quiet Corner Rest Home."

She waggled her eyebrows at Neil and mouthed the words *Quiet Corner* and *Rest* at him as if she could hardly believe them. In spite of himself, Neil grinned.

"You are speaking to Miss Primrose Cobham, long-standing resident of this establishment." Miss Cobham tucked the handset under her chin, tightened the belt of her blue dressing gown and took a firmer grip on her walking frame. "Now, if you MUST call at this time of day, how may I help you? Oh, Mr Loftus, it's you."

"I said it was," said Mum, appearing at her elbow and taking the phone from her. "I told you, Neil, it was only Dad. And I'd be grateful, Miss Cobham, if you'd leave the phone to me. Now, Jim, what is it this time?"

As she listened, she made shooing movements at Miss Cobham and Neil to go away. Neither of them went. Neil was trying to hear what Dad was saying. He sounded very distant. Actually, he was just round the corner, calling from his tiny flat in the next road.

"No," Mum kept saying. "No need for that, Jim. I can manage perfectly well. I've got plenty of help. No, thank you. No."

Dad, thought Neil. Yet again Dad was offering to come round and help.

Once, Dad and Mum had worked together running the Quiet Corner Rest Home. But that had been before the divorce. Now Mum ran the home on her own and Dad was supposed to have his own job as a taxi driver. But he just couldn't stay away from the Quiet Corner Rest Home.

"What?" said Mum. "Who?"

Neil took a step closer.

"Oh, right," said Mum, smiling suddenly. "You know you can, Jim, any time. He's here." She held out the phone to Neil. "It's Dad, dear. For you."

She spoke in her special sugary voice. It was the voice she used when she told people how nice it was for Neil that Dad lived just round the corner, and how well Neil was coping with the divorce.

Mum, thought Neil, and took the phone.

"Hi, Dad."

"Hello, Neil."

Neil listened, watching Mum steer Miss Cobham back to her room and then go downstairs to see to the breakfasts. He glanced at his watch. There wasn't much time, he thought. There were plenty of trains on the London Underground in the rush hour, but he knew he mustn't arrive late at school this morning. His form teacher wanted to see him first thing.

Dad was asking Neil to come round to his flat after school, to do his homework there and have tea.

"OK, Dad. Thanks."

He wouldn't go, of course. He'd have to think of an excuse by this afternoon and ring him from home. He wouldn't go because Dad would start looking at the homework, offering to help him. Then Dad would find out how little Neil knew, how little he understood of anything he was supposed to be doing since he'd started at his new school.

"You can always pop in to see me, Neil. Any time you like."

Dad's special voice wasn't sugary like Mum's. It was just hopeful.

"And your friends. Why not bring a couple of your friends round today?"

"All right."

As Dad talked on and on, Neil twisted round to look through the open door of Miss Cobham's room. Her walls were lined with posters.

'SAIL THE WORLD WITH THE RANGOLD LINE,' read the poster nearest Neil. 'WE MAKE ALL YOUR DREAMS COME TRUE.'

On the poster a man and a woman in old-fashioned evening clothes leaned over the rail of an ocean liner. In the night sky over their heads hung a big golden moon.

What friends? thought Neil. *I haven't got any friends.*

It was just after this that the fax came.

2

He was in the office next to the dining room when it came.

He'd fetched himself a bowl of cereal and was scooping at it and following Mum around as she sorted out papers and made lists. Through the open hatch he could see the residents sitting at their tables. Carol, one of Mum's assistants, was ladling out porridge. Across the room, Neil saw Dad pushing Mr Parsons along in his wheelchair. So Dad had come round to help, just as Neil had known he would.

"Mum, please."

He was trying to get her to give him some money. He was supposed to be going on a school holiday to Norfolk in the spring and he'd just remembered he had to pay in the last of the money today.

"In a minute, Neil," said Mum. "I'll need my cheque book. See if you can find it."

He was starting to look for it when the fax machine on

the desk gave a croak. Mum looked at it crossly. "A fax coming through," she said. "That's all I need. I hope it's nothing important. I've got the nurse coming this morning to do Miss Cobham's legs and . . ." She looked out of the window. "Oh, help, here's the man to mend the tumble dryer. You'd better ask your father for that money."

"Mum –"

But she'd gone.

Neil turned and watched the fax machine. The printer was whirring and clicking. A length of paper was slowly unrolling as the message was printed out.

The first thing he saw at the top of the paper was two slender waving tentacles. As he watched, fascinated, the rest of the drawing emerged, millimetre by millimetre. He saw that the tentacles belonged to a crab, a crab waving its tentacles from inside a spiral seashell much too small for it.

Underneath the drawing of the crab was a name and an address:

Tessa Loftus,
The Hermit Shell,
Ship Street,
Portmartin,
Cornwall.

So his Aunt Tessa was back in the country. She'd been abroad for so long that he had almost forgotten she existed.

"Good grief," said Dad, coming in and leaning over Neil's shoulder. "So my sister's surfaced again. I thought

14

she was in Nepal or somewhere. What's she doing in Cornwall?"

"Still painting," said Neil, reading the message in its black stylish handwriting. He knew his Aunt Tessa was an artist but he couldn't remember what she looked like. He did remember that once, a long time ago, he'd spoken to her on the telephone. Every now and then, a postcard would come from her, from Bali, from Mexico, from Nepal. Just once, although it wasn't his birthday, she'd sent him a present: a tiny, heavy brass frog.

"Look, she says she's having something called a One-Woman Show. An exhibition of her paintings and stuff. And she's inviting you and Mum to go down to Cornwall and see it."

Dad straightened up.

"Yes, well," he said. "I don't think that's on. Tessa's got a lot of catching up to do. Now, about this school holiday money . . ." He took out his wallet.

Neil was still looking at the crab waving its tentacles at the top of the paper.

"The Hermit Shell," he said. "I wonder why her house is called The Hermit Shell."

3

"Neil! Where are you? You're going to be late."

Neil opened the door of Room 6.

"I'm in here, Mum."

"Miss Cobham doesn't want you there in her room,"

said Mum. "She's got the nurse coming in a minute."

"OK, I'm going in a sec." He had completely forgotten he had to get to school on time today.

He shut the door again and went back to the book he and Miss Cobham had been studying.

As well as posters, her room was full of books, nearly all of them about the sea. When she'd been younger, Miss Cobham had been a stewardess with the Rangold Line and she had crossed the Atlantic two hundred and thirty-eight times.

"I bet I'm right," she said.

"Yes, you are," said Neil. "That crab on the fax – it's a hermit crab, Pag-u-rus bern . . . bernhardus, the Common Hermit Crab. Look, it's got all this hard armour at the front, but its back half is quite soft and it says here it's always afraid enemies are going to get it from behind. So it looks for an empty shell, and as soon as it finds one –"

"Zoom," said Miss Cobham. "It's in."

"Backwards. Like backing into a parking space."

"And there it is in its new home."

"Holding the entrance shut with its claw," said Neil.

"Lucky devil," said Miss Cobham feelingly. "No phone screeching outside its door first thing in the morning. No boring, boring meals for it to sit through. No nurses coming to unwind all its bandages and wind them up again . . ." She looked down angrily at her swollen feet in their thick red socks and shapeless slippers.

"No anything," said Neil. "Just cruising round the bottom of the sea, holding the entrance shut and waving your tentacles."

For a second he was that crab, curled inside that whelk shell, safe from the world. The book said that the hermit crab held on tightly to the walls inside the shell with special foot-like suckers.

"When I was a girl, and we went on holiday," Miss Cobham said dreamily, "there'd be crabs in the rock-pools. I'd lie face down on the beach, dabbling in the water, looking for crabs."

"Where?" asked Neil.

"Cornwall. Like your Aunt Tessa. But that was yonks ago." Miss Cobham sighed. "Yonks. I wish I could –"

"What?"

"Head off down there this minute," said Miss Cobham. "Get on the train at Paddington and off right at the end of England. All the way down to the far west. I want to see the Atlantic again, not all this London stuff. I want to smell the waves, the spray, not all this . . . this talcum powder and air freshener."

She screwed up her face in disgust. Then she looked at Neil fiercely.

"The sun always shone in Cornwall, you know."

"Did it?"

Miss Cobham glared out at the street where the nurse was just parking her car.

"No, of course it didn't. Just felt like it, because I was young. Young and happy."

"NEIL!"

Miss Cobham took the book away from Neil and tucked it back on its shelf.

"That's your mum," she said.

She looked at him. Her eyes were very blue behind her thick glasses.

"You're all right, are you?" she asked.

"Yes," said Neil. "Why not?"

"No reason," said Miss Cobham. "No reason at all. I heard your mother saying only yesterday how well you're coping with things. And I said to myself: bully for old Neil. Now –" She propelled him to the door. "Go. And have a good day."

She gave a short laugh.

"If that's at all possible."

4

The Underground train was absolutely packed.

Neil stood with dozens of other people bunched around the doors, all of them swaying and lurching together as the train rattled along in the dark. He could hardly breathe. His face was wedged against a woman's shoulder, and someone's briefcase was jammed into the back of his knees. He twisted sideways to look at the window and glimpsed his own face, like a ghost face, reflected in the grey, curved tunnel wall that was swooping along just the other side of the glass.

There was a squeal of brakes and then sudden, brilliant light as the train pulled into a station. The doors slid open.

"MIND THE GAP," intoned the recorded voice. "MIND THE GAP."

The briefcase banged Neil's leg one last time as its

owner pushed past. People struggled out onto the platform and others surged in.

"Hey, look who's here." Two boys squeezed through the doors just before they closed. "It's little Nelly Loftus!"

"How you doing, Nelly?"

Neil went rigid. If only he'd caught an earlier train. He looked away, feeling his face go hot and red. The train slid out of the station and plunged into the dark again, picking up speed.

"What's the matter with Nelly?" asked Martyn Rossal. He passed his hand up and down in front of Neil's eyes. His school tie hung loose and crooked. "Gone to sleep, has she?"

Lee Takiendis laughed. "No, she's still in there somewhere. Aren't you, Nelly?"

He jiggled about and pulled his fingers to make them crack. Neil jumped, in spite of himself.

"Told you she was awake," said Lee. "Hi ya, Nelly."

Sometimes, at home in bed for instance, Neil thought about Martyn and Lee and he imagined himself standing up to them.

"Get lost," he'd say to them. "Get lost and don't pick on me. I'm not interested in the rubbish you talk."

He'd say it and they'd stop at once, open-mouthed in surprise. "You bullies," he'd say. "I'm reporting you."

And he would report them. He'd tell a teacher. He'd tell the special Bullying Council that had recently been set up at school. Then it would stop.

But was it bullying?

Perhaps it wasn't real bullying at all. Perhaps it wasn't

anything much. All the two boys did was called Neil . . .
that name. Nelly. Pretending he was a girl called Nelly.
They did it on the train, or in odd corners of the school
when nobody else was listening, or on the way to the
station in the afternoons.

What had made them start it? It must have been
something about him. They'd begun almost as soon as
Neil met them, when he moved up to the big school. His
primary school friends had all gone to a different school.
And, because Martyn and Lee called him that name, quite
a lot of other kids began to copy them. And now Neil was
stuck with it.

The train came into another station. More people
squeezed off and on. Neil was pressed closer to Martyn
and Lee.

"Looking forward to the trip, Nelly?" asked Lee. "You
know, the school trip to Norfolk?"

Neil nodded, warily, and wedged his school bag tighter
between his feet. "We're looking forward to it too," said
Lee. "Aren't we, Martyn?"

"Yeah," said Martyn. "I'm paying in my money today.
Got the cheque here." He opened his school bag and
showed Neil a brown envelope.

Neil looked at the envelope.

"You two aren't going on that holiday," he said. He was
starting to shake inside. "Your names weren't on the list."
That was why Neil wanted to go. He'd have a whole week
away from Martyn and Lee.

"We changed our minds," said Martyn. "Got a right to,
haven't we? It'll be a good laugh up there in Norfolk.

Us and you, Nelly, and the rest of the kids."

The brakes screeched and the train began to slow down again. There were still two more stations before theirs.

"MIND THE GAP. MIND THE GAP."

People pushed past them, getting off, getting on.

"We'll be company for you, Nelly." said Lee. "Stop you getting homesick."

The doors began to slide shut.

Neil didn't think about it at all. He simply picked up his bag and stepped out onto the platform. The doors closed.

For a second, he saw two astonished faces pressed to the glass, mouthing something to him.

Then the train pulled away, and rattled into the dark tunnel and was gone.

There was a sudden silence.

Neil stood completely still. People were milling all around him, hurrying to the escalators.

Over his head, an indicator board flashed, showing another train due in two minutes.

So everything could still be all right. He could get on the next train and be whisked off to school as if nothing had happened. But then he'd have to get through the day. He'd have to see his form teacher and he was already late. He'd have to hear Martyn and Lee shouting out that name, telling everyone how he had got off the train at the wrong station. He'd have to sit through lessons he didn't understand.

Then either he *wouldn't* go to tea with Dad, and Dad

would be hurt. Or he *would* go to tea with Dad, and Mum would be cross. For Neil was never taken in by Mum's sugary voice. Underneath, whenever Neil spent time with Dad, Mum was cross.

He glanced up at the indicator board. One minute to the next train.

The hermit crab, he thought, holds on tightly to the walls inside the shell with special foot-like suckers. It keeps the entrance shut with its claw.

That's what he needed. He needed a place of his own away from everything, somewhere with an entrance he could keep shut.

The train came in. He turned his back on it and faced the wall. He found he was staring at a plan of the London Underground system. He ran his finger over its familiar multicoloured lines, located the yellow Circle Line, traced it round to its top left corner, and there was the word 'PADDINGTON'.

5

It was easy. So easy.

He felt completely calm.

First he went up the escalator to the surface where the ticket machines were and bought a ticket to Paddington. Then he went back down to the tunnels. He caught first one train to switch onto the Circle Line, and then another straight through to Paddington.

By the time the second train arrived, the rush to work

was over and there were plenty of seats on it. He sat still, using the short journey to plan.

He had plenty of money. Dad hadn't wanted to give him the holiday money in cash, but he hadn't got his cheque book with him that morning.

"Look, for goodness sake be careful," he'd said, fishing out banknotes from his taxi money and sealing them in an envelope he addressed to Neil's form teacher. "Remember all the muggers around. Put this money right at the bottom of your bag, and don't take it out at all till you reach school. Promise, now."

Neil had promised. But now he knew Martyn and Lee were going on the holiday, everything was different.

"MIND THE GAP. MIND THE GAP."

He was at Paddington. Half the passengers in the carriage stood up to leave. Neil went with them, hurrying along the platform, sailing up on escalators, following signs to the mainline station.

Then he was climbing up into the station concourse, echoing and airy after the stuffiness of the underground, and the time on the station clock was 9.40.

Staring at the clock he felt, just for a moment, a flick of fear. He'd missed the appointment with his form teacher. He'd missed answering his name at registration. He would have been marked absent by now, and his class would be halfway through a maths lesson.

He shook his head, pushing the thoughts away, and went to look for the booking office. While he waited in line, he took the envelope of money out of his bag.

"Next?"

23

It was his turn. He took a deep breath.

"Um . . . Cornwall," he said. "Please."

The clerk looked at him.

"Where in Cornwall?"

Why hadn't he found out the name of a station?

"As far as the train goes," he said, hearing an echo of Miss Cobham's voice that morning. "All the way."

He made himself meet the clerk's eyes, opened the envelope and took out some money.

That seemed to reassure her in some way.

"Penzance?" She began to tap on a keyboard.

"That's right." He didn't know if it was or not.

"Single or return?"

After a moment's hesitation, Neil said, "Single," and pushed a handful of money under the glass.

"Single to Penzance."

The ticket came spinning back to him.

"*Cornish Riviera*," said the clerk. "That's the train you want. Going at 10.35. Next."

Neil went off to wait.

He perched on his bag, glancing up every few minutes at the giant indicator board, waiting for the *Cornish Riviera* to be announced. Then his heart gave a jump. Two policewomen were coming towards him, scanning the crowds.

It wasn't possible they could be searching for him. But they might be looking for school truants. They just might be.

As casually as he could, he slipped off his school tie and

then shuffled closer to a young couple and their little boy. He kept his head down as the policewomen went past and they took no notice of him. To them he must have seemed part of the family.

When at last the *Cornish Riviera* came up on the board, he showed his ticket at the barrier and walked a long way down the platform beside the waiting carriages. He glanced back once over his shoulder. Then he climbed into the train.

All around him people were taking off coats, stowing bags on racks and settling down in their seats. Hardly anyone else was alone. But that was all right. The hermit crab was alone in its shell.

There was a clock outside the window. He sat watching the figures ticking away: 10.34 and 40 seconds . . . 50 seconds . . . 10.35 . . . 10.35 and 10 seconds . . . 20 –

A whistle blew, the train gave a small jerk and the platform began to slide past the window.

He was on his way.

6

It was around that time, three hundred miles to the west, that Tessa Loftus looked up from the picture she was painting and glanced out of her window.

"Rain," she said, absently cleaning her paint brush on a rag and wiping her hands down her paint-spattered trousers. "It's going to rain later on. I just know it. And I'm going out before it starts."

After nearly a year in Cornwall, Tessa knew the signs. There was a soft January blue sky arching over the sea, with only two or three innocent-looking wisps of white cloud floating in it. But the wind this morning was the sort of wind that would get up and bring rain. These small clouds would join forces, they'd spread and become a thick, grey mass that blotted out the sun. And then it would rain, perhaps for hours.

Five minutes later she stood on her doorstep, pulling on her boots and picking up her red plastic bucket. She often took a bucket on her beach walks. She liked to bring back interesting things.

She locked her front door and pocketed the key. Then she stood on the doorstep for a moment, as she often did, looking up at her small house. She could hear a gull on the roof screeching, and the waves just behind the house lapping on the rocks.

The Hermit Shell, she thought fondly. And it's all mine. After years of wandering round the world with nowhere to call her own, she could still hardly believe it. Her own house, bought with her own money. OK, it may be the smallest house in Portmartin, perhaps in the whole of Cornwall. But it was hers.

She went round the side of the house, pulling up her jacket collar against the freshening wind. She climbed over the low stone wall that separated her little back garden from the beach. On the other side of the wall, stained concrete steps led down over the rocks to the clean sand that was only uncovered when the tide was low, as it was this morning.

26

She walked along the sand, swinging her bucket, humming to herself. After a few minutes she drew level with the steps up to the harbour wall. She could see Portmartin's lifeboat station from there, and the letters 'RNLI' on the flag flapping from the roof. The boat had been wheeled out of doors. Mat Boswell, the coxswain and mechanic, was up on deck.

"Mat," she called. "Hello, Mat."

"Morning, Tess!" Mat waved back. "Coming up?"

Tessa shook her head, laughing and pointing at the sky. She waved the bucket to show she was off on a long walk. Then she turned and headed into the wind, leaving a line of footprints along the edge of the sea.

CHAPTER TWO

The End of England

"PENZANCE. This is PENZANCE . . ."

The *Cornish Riviera* had arrived.

Neil jumped down to the platform. He hurried along with the rest of the passengers, rain spattering their faces, all of them seeking the shelter of the station glass roof.

It had started raining soon after they left Exeter, about the time Neil was eating the school sandwiches he'd fished from his bag. By the time they'd stopped in Plymouth, before they crossed the long bridge into Cornwall, rain was lashing the windows and a thick blanket of cloud blotted out most of the scenery. He'd dozed for a while then, only half aware that they were stopping more often now: St Austell . . . Redruth . . . St Erth . . .

And at last, after all those hours in the train, Penzance. This was where the railway line finished. Going out of the station, he stopped for a moment to stare at a large granite boulder. It was set across the end of the rail tracks, blocking trains from going any further. The words 'Penzance welcomes you' were carved on it and, underneath, 'PENSANS A'GAS DYNERGH'. What language was that? he wondered. Whatever it was, it was clear he'd reached the end of England that Miss Cobham had talked about.

He stood outside the station, hunched against the rain and wind, looking round. At least there was none of the stale cotton wool feel of London air.

Where now? he thought. How was he to get to Portmartin?

He looked across the station yard and thought he could make out the masts of ships and what looked like palm trees. He bent his head into the rain and set off towards them. Then he noticed a bus station to the left and veered over that way.

There were a few people queueing. Only one bus was waiting. He walked round it to look. On the front was the single name 'Portmartin'.

Could it be that simple, a bus just standing there, waiting for him?

Apparently it was.

"Just leaving," the driver said when Neil asked when he was going.

So he paid the fare and found a seat near the back. And within a minute the bus started up and went.

That proves it, Neil thought. I was meant to come here.
I knew I was.

2

He wiped a circle on the clouded window and looked out.
The bus was splashing down a narrow street crowded with
shoppers. In a way it was just like home; he saw
Woolworths, Boots, Barclays Bank. But then they came to
the sea front and he saw a line of palm trees, and boats
with tall masts and the whole misty sweep of a bay. And
suddenly it was nothing like London at all.

They stopped outside a school and a group of children
piled on, filling all the remaining seats. They were all
talking and laughing, and Neil could almost pretend he
was one of them. Almost but not quite. This school
uniform was different. So were the soft Cornish accents.

"Anyone got a clue what that physics lesson was
about?" a girl behind Neil was demanding. "I'm never
going to get the homework done."

"I'll show you," said Neil's neighbour. She swung
round, her hair falling over her face, took an exercise book
out of her bag and started to explain something. The other
girl shook her head.

"I haven't got a clue," she kept saying. "Oh, I haven't got
a clue, Annis."

Neil wiped the window again. They were passing
through a village now. The road was so narrow that twice

they had to stop while cars reversed to make way for them. He realised with a shock that evening was closing in, that lights were coming on.

He ought to be at Dad's flat by now, having tea and doing his homework. He imagined Dad sitting there, waiting for him. What would he do when Neil didn't turn up? Phone Mum, probably.

The bus slowed down. The girl behind him got up.

"See you, Annis, then."

"Bye," said Annis. "You all right with that homework?"

The other girl spread her hands and laughed again.

"Ta anyway," she said, and moved on down the bus. She jumped down and the bus went on, twisting and turning. In a few minutes, Neil saw a signpost saying 'Portmartin 1'. Almost at once they were travelling steeply downhill with the lights of a village below them.

They stopped in a square. Neil saw white stone houses with grey slate roofs, a grey chapel with a little pointed steeple, a General Store with a red and white striped blind that had rain dripping off it.

Most people got out here. Neil hesitated, but the bus was already starting up again. He and the girl called Annis were the only two left on board now.

They drove down a street so narrow that the few people out walking had to flatten themselves against the wall as the bus squeezed past them. Neil could see right into the front rooms of the houses they passed.

Then they turned a corner. The engine gave one more roar and fell silent. The driver glanced round at them.

Neil followed Annis to the door.

"Thank you," she called to the driver. "Bye."

"Thanks," muttered Neil, a bit awkwardly. He wasn't used to thanking London bus drivers.

He paused on the steps. A fresh wind was gusting in his face.

Fish, he thought, sniffing. A strong smell of quite old fish and rain and . . . was that roaring noise the sea?

He dropped down to the road and found himself by Portmartin harbour.

3

No wonder they'd stopped. The road didn't go any further. Already the driver was turning the bus round to go back to Penzance.

Neil leaned over the harbour rail, feeling the rain spattering his shoulders. The black water seemed a long way down, sliding and slurping. Small boats bobbed and jostled on their ropes. He heard the sound of an engine, and looked up to see a fishing boat gliding in through a gap in the massive sea walls, lights high on its mast, sea birds crying round its decks.

This is good, he thought. It's really good.

He straightened up. Behind him the village rose up the hillside, roof upon roof, lights twinkling. The girl called Annis was just crossing the road, her school bag under her arm. He ran after her.

"Excuse me."

She turned round. They were standing outside a gift

shop. The only things in its window were a few faded postcards, a dummy packet of Cornish Fudge lying in a corner, and a handwritten sign saying 'Open at Easter'.

"Yes?" She slowed down a bit but went on walking, head bent into the wind, her dark hair blown back from her face. She was taller than he was, he realised.

Neil hurried to keep up with her. "I'm looking for Ship Street," he said.

The girl looked at him.

"It's over there." She pointed. "Round the harbour, nearly as far as the sea, then first left. You can't miss it."

"OK, thanks," said Neil. He cleared his throat. "This looks like a nice place."

She smiled. "Yes, it is. Look, I've got to go in here. I've just seen my dad inside."

"Oh, right," said Neil.

She'd stopped outside the window of a blue-painted café called Penna's. There were lights behind the steamy window and he caught a glimpse of a couple at a table in the window, talking. The man, big, fair-haired, saw Annis and waved.

"He usually has a break about now," she said. "If he's not out on a shout. Bye."

She went into the café and shut the door. Someone had left a long piece of wood on the doorstep, and a red bucket full of seaweed.

Neil went on round the harbour, the wind whipping at his clothes, the rain spattering his face.

Out on a shout, he thought. *What's that?* Then he forgot about it because his heart was beginning to pound in his chest. He could hear Miss Cobham's voice saying, "Right to the end of England," and "Bully for old Neil." And he remembered her poster: WE MAKE ALL YOUR DREAMS COME TRUE. But that had been far away and long, long ago this morning.

He reached the turning on the left and started to climb Ship Street. It was very narrow. The houses stared straight across at each other and it didn't need the double yellow lines to tell you not to park there. If you did, you'd block the street.

The houses had names like 'Spindrift' and 'Trewartha' and 'St Just'. By the time Neil reached the top of the street he'd almost given up hope of finding The Hermit Shell.

But it was there. A tall, very narrow cottage, the last one on the right. It was painted white, and it had only two windows, one above the other. The front door was of polished wood and made in two halves like a stable door. By the door, on the white wall, someone had painted 'The Hermit Shell' in curly black writing and, under that, in pink, the same hermit crab that had come winding out of Mum's fax machine that morning.

Neil put down his bag. Now he was actually here, he didn't feel anything: not excited, not nervous or frightened. Not anything.

He tapped with the knocker and waited, wiping the rain from his face. The roar of the sea was louder here.

No-one came.

He knocked again louder.

Of course. He realised he wasn't thinking very straight. The windows were dark. He peered through the downstairs one and saw plants on the window-sill and pictures on the walls, a sofa, a table and a dresser. Everything seemed to be covered in papers and books. There was a fireplace with a fire laid in it, all ready to light.

He set off round the end wall to look at the back of the house. Before he'd gone two steps, the wind and the rain struck him full in the face. The sea was roaring, smashing again and again somewhere just below the house, and he was blinded and deafened. He just glimpsed a little square garden with a low stone wall, saw there was no light from the rear windows either, and then struggled back to the front again.

He sank down on the front doorstep. His legs had no more strength in them. He'd come all this way and now he couldn't get in. He was cold and hungry, tired and very wet.

He sat hugging his bag, his head on his knees. He couldn't think of anything else to do but to sit there and wait till something happened.

4

"Hello," said a voice. "You all right down there?"

Neil looked up.

A woman was standing there, a woman with a lot of wet dark hair. His Aunt Tessa. It must be.

"Are you the boy who was looking for Ship Street?"

She put down her red plastic bucket, propped up the long piece of wood she'd been carrying and began searching her pockets.

"Annis mentioned you to Mat and me just now in the café."

She took out her key and looked down at Neil again.

"Are you OK?" she asked. She smiled down at him, but it was the blank, polite smile of a stranger.

Neil's stomach turned over. She didn't know who he was. Any minute now she might step round him and vanish into the house. He said the first silly thing that came into his head, anything to stop her shutting the door on him.

"What's in that bucket?"

She turned round.

"Dead Men's Ropes," she said. "Nice name. Do you want to see?"

He nodded. She tilted the bucket so the street light fell on it and scooped up a handful of slippery brown seaweed strands.

"I think I'm going to have something like it in my next painting," she said. "And this piece of wood. I picked it up this morning on the beach, and it reminded me of an antler, a stag's antler. What do you think?"

The wood forked into two pointed tapering shapes. Just for a moment, Neil saw what she meant.

"It's going to be a forest picture," she went on, "a sea forest."

She smiled again at him. This time it was more friendly. "Where are you going?" she said, "I'd hurry along now and get into the dry. You look terribly wet."

"But I'm Neil," he said.

"What?" She stared at him.

"Neil." This was awful. He licked his lips and they tasted of salt. "Neil Loftus. You're my aunt. I – I left this morning. I've got away. I've just arrived. I –"

"Neil," she said. "You're Jim's boy. From London."

"Yes," said Neil.

"Look," she said, "we're both getting soaked. Come inside a minute."

She pushed open the door and he followed her into the house. He was inside the living room he'd seen through the window. Stairs led straight up at one side of it.

"Right." She took the bucket through to the kitchen and came back with a towel. "Here. Catch."

He caught it.

"Take off that wet jacket." She was filling the kettle, lifting down two mugs. "Dry your face and hair."

He obeyed, dropping his jacket on the floor, wiping his face. Over the towel he watched her putting a match to the fire. Then she went through to make the tea.

He stood by the fire. In a minute or so she came back and handed him a steaming mug of tea. Then she stood staring at him.

"I thought you were about seven," she said. "I hadn't realised . . . Jim and I haven't seen much of each other for years."

"I know."

"Let's get this straight," she said slowly. "You left London this morning, to come down here."

He nodded, wrapping his hands round the hot mug.

"And your mum and dad?" she said. "Do they know about this?"

Her green eyes were very direct. He shook his head, looking away from her.

"No. I – I saw this shell, you see, this hermit shell on your fax . . . On the fax paper . . ." The words were getting stuck in his chest. "There was this crab, and Miss Cobham said – said you could zoom in and close the entrance and people would leave you alone . . ."

"You wanted people to leave you alone?"

He nodded. "I wanted to come here," he said. "To The Hermit Shell. I thought I'd be safe here."

"But it's mine," she said. "My house."

"I know." There was a hard lump in his throat. "I – I didn't think about it being yours or anything. I just wanted to . . ."

He came to a stop, staring out of the window.

After a moment she said,

"Look, Neil. I probably haven't understood much of this. But I think I've got one thing. Your parents don't know where you are. Nobody does. Yes?"

"Yes." He blew his nose.

"Right." She picked up the phone.

"Don't ring them. I –"

She lowered the phone. "Neil," she said, "your parents must be worried sick by now, wondering what's happened to you. I must ring them. What's their number? I always have to look it up."

After a minute, he told her the number. She keyed it in and sat on the bottom stair, waiting for an answer. He stood awkwardly, watching.

"Hello? Could I speak to – Sorry, who's that? Primrose who?"

Neil started to say something.

"Hang on a minute," said Tessa. She put her hand over the mouthpiece. "Why don't you have a hot shower, Neil, while I'm doing this? It's through there, over in the corner." She nodded towards the kitchen.

As he went, he heard her say,

"Right. Well, could you get Mr or Mrs Loftus to the phone, please? It's rather urgent. Tell them I've got their son Neil here with me. In Cornwall."

Neil just heard a squawk at the other end of the line. Then he was inside a tiny whitewashed bathroom with the door shut.

Once the shower was running he tried to picture what was happening at home. But it was too complicated, too far away, and he let it all wash away with the stream of hot, comforting water cascading over his cold body.

By the time he came out, the towel round his middle, she was just finishing the conversation.

"Yes, I will, Jim, that's fine. Try not to worry. Bye, now."

She put down the phone.

"Your parents are coming down tomorrow," she said.

"Together?" he asked, startled.

"Yes."

"Why?" Though he knew the answer.

She looked at him. "To take you back to London," she said. "They were – I just had a quick word with them both. Luckily, your dad was there, though I gather he doesn't live there any more. Is that right?"

"They got divorced," said Neil. "Last year."

"I didn't know they'd split up for good," she said. "I'm sorry, Neil. Anyway, he was there, hunting for you because you hadn't turned up for tea at his place. They were worried out of their minds, Neil. They were just about to call the police. They were so relieved . . . When I said you were in Cornwall they couldn't believe it." She shook her head, gazing at him as if she couldn't believe it either. "Anyway, they're coming tomorrow."

He stared at his bare feet. "Do they have to?"

There was a silence. He could feel her looking at him.

"Neil," she said at last, "I'm sorry if you're having problems. Truly I am. But I can't see how coming down here would help."

"I want to live here," he said stubbornly.

"But –" said Tessa. "I live here, and I like living alone. There really isn't room for two. Anyway, Neil, you'd be bored in a week."

"I wouldn't." He thought of how happy he'd felt when he'd stepped off the bus and found himself by the harbour, of how that fishing boat had looked, coming in with lights on its mast. "I wouldn't."

They stared at each other. Then Tessa sighed.

"OK, let's leave it there. I'll get you some clothes and we'll have a meal. Goodness knows what." She looked round helplessly. "Then bed. We won't think about it until tomorrow. Is that all right, Neil?"

40

5

Neil woke only once that night.

Huddled in blankets on Tessa's sofa, he'd been deeply asleep when the footsteps came running past the window. Someone pounded on the front door.

"Tess! Annis is on her way, love. It's a shout."

"Right. I'll let her in."

He struggled up on his elbow. He saw the pale wedge of the open front door and felt a rush of cold air. Then Tessa was coming back inside, talking quietly to a small shape beside her.

He was half dazed with sleep.

"What's a shout?" he murmured.

"Shh, Neil," whispered Tessa. "Go back to sleep."

"But what is it?"

"It's when the lifeboat's called out. Annis has come over to us till her dad gets back, that's all."

The two shapes tiptoed up the stairs.

Neil turned over. Just before he swam down into sleep again he thought he heard Annis say,

"Will it be all right?"

and Tessa answer,

"Yes. It always is and it will be this time."

CHAPTER THREE

All Your Dreams Come True

It was the seagulls that finally woke Neil on Saturday morning.

He opened his eyes and, somewhere just outside, seagulls were screeching. Now he was awake he couldn't think how he could have slept through the noise. He sat up and lifted the curtain by his head. The street outside was in deep shadow and the road still looked wet. The house opposite was so near you could almost reach out and touch its yellow shutters. There were two large white seagulls perched on its roof, necks stretched out, screaming at each other.

He pushed back the blankets and padded across the cold room. The fire had died to ashes, but his clothes felt dry. Just as he reached the kitchen door, Tessa came out of the bathroom.

"Morning, Neil." She was wrapped in a dressing gown. "Sleep all right?"

"Yes thanks, Auntie Tessa."

She winced. "Just Tessa will do," she said. "I'll be upstairs getting some painting done if you want me. Make yourself some tea or something if you like. OK?"

"OK." Neil flattened himself against the wall to let her reach the stairs. Then he opened the kitchen door and was nearly drowned in light.

Last night's wind and rain had completely gone. There seemed to be nothing outside the back window but sky and sea and sun.

For a moment, he just stared. Then he unlocked the back door and went out. The sharp winter air stung his face, and the stone path was icy under his bare feet, but he took no notice. He crossed the little back garden and leaned over the wall.

Below him were glistening wet rocks, and a wide stretch of empty yellow sand running out to the sea. Miles and miles of sea all the way to the horizon.

He drew a deep breath. Across the bay on one side the sun was just rising over the bare headland. He squinted at it and its rays shimmered on the water, dazzling him. Round to his other side two small fishing boats were coming out of the harbour, bobbing along one behind the other. The putter of their engines reached him on the morning air, mingling with the soft sound of turning waves. Over it all, the gulls circled and squabbled and called.

Arriving in the dark last night, he'd had no idea. But this morning he could see. The Hermit Shell was built right on the rocks, right above the beach.

"It's ... It's ... " he started to say. He couldn't find words for it, for anything quite so wonderful. He just couldn't take in all that space, all that light, all that sea.

2

He got dressed and made some tea and then hung around, not knowing what to do. He could hear Tessa moving about upstairs but she didn't come down. And where was Annis?

At last he went up to see what was going on. He stood on the top stair and put his head round the door.

The room beyond was big, running from front to back of the house. It smelled of paint and wood and turpentine. All round the walls were shelves, some holding paint tubes and brushes, some piled high with books. Boards and canvases were stacked on the bare polished floor. In one corner was a neatly made bed with a blue and gold cover and a pile of cushions and blankets on the floor. Annis must have gone back to her own house while he was still asleep.

Tessa was in the middle of the room, standing at an easel, painting. She was wearing a thick plaid top over

44

paint-spattered jeans and a blue scarf round her neck. The window was wide open and it was icy cold. She saw him and laid down her brush.

"Oh, Neil, I'm sorry, I've forgotten all about you," she said. "I was painting and . . . Are you OK?"

"I'm fine," said Neil.

"Look, we'll go out later." She picked up a half-eaten apple and took a bite. "When I've done a bit more on this. Or you could go and have a look round Portmartin on your own."

He considered this for a moment. In London, he didn't go out much on his own except to go to school.

"All right."

"As long as you stay in the village. I'll meet you by the harbour at – what? – eleven o'clock. Have you got a watch? Good."

She smiled at him and picked up her brush. Then she lowered it again.

"Is there anything else?" She raised an eyebrow at him. "Take an apple from the dish if you want one."

He took one. "Thanks."

Just as he was going, she said, "You seem quite sensible. You aren't going to do anything silly, are you?"

"No." He smiled back, a bit uncertainly.

"I'm sure you aren't," she said. "Take care, and I'll see you later."

She went back to her painting. Neil retreated, carrying his apple downstairs. For a place where all his dreams were supposed to come true, he reflected, there didn't seem to be a lot of food around.

He walked along the beach, biting at the apple. His shoes sank slightly into the damp sand at every step and his breath steamed.

He turned and looked back at The Hermit Shell. From here he could see there was an extra window jutting out from the roof, facing straight out to sea. What a view there'd be from up there, he thought.

At the end of the beach he climbed the steps to the harbour. Directly ahead was a large building. Its big double doors stood open and he saw a boat inside. It was standing high on a carriage, its bows pointing towards the sea.

He stood by the doors for a moment, looking in. A notice board told him that this was the lifeboat and it was called *Dolly Hescomb*, and that she had a crew of six. Their names were listed, and their phone numbers. The first name on the list was 'M. Boswell (Coxswain/ Mechanic)'.

"Hello."

Neil turned round. It was the girl from last night, Annis.

"Hi."

She was wearing orange boots and black trousers and an orange lifejacket over her white sweater.

"It was you who came in last night," he said.

She nodded. "Sorry if I woke you up. My dad and I live opposite Tessa, in the house with yellow shutters. Dad's pager went off just as he was going to bed –"

"Pager?"

"His electronic bleeper," she explained. "He takes it

everywhere with him in case there's a call to take the lifeboat out."

"A shout," said Neil. "It's called a shout."

"That's right," said Annis. "Dad's the cox of the crew. Mat Boswell. All the crew have pagers and when they hear a bleep they drop everything and run. Since – since my mum died, I always go over to Tessa's when there's a shout."

"Yes, I see," said Neil. "Why was the boat called out last night?"

"They took the doctor out to a coaster," she said. "There was a man on board they thought had had a heart attack. But he hadn't, so that was all right. Except my dad and the rest didn't get much sleep last night. Still, they're used to that. I'm just waiting for Dad now. He's in the office. He's the mechanic as well as the cox so he works here full-time."

"Right."

Neil wandered round, looking up at the polished blue and white sides of the boat. Then he climbed the viewing platform to see the deck and look into the wheelhouse with its heavy watertight door. Inside there, it looked more like the flight deck of an airliner than a boat; there were complicated-looking dials and two big pilot's seats But out on deck it would be different. He tried to imagine being out in a storm on a dark night, with the waves crashing and water pouring over everything.

He went down again and saw the crew's waterproof jackets, trousers and sea boots, lined up ready to be put on quickly. And there was a shiny brass plaque on the wall.

He started to read it and found it was a memorial for a lifeboat, lost twenty-five years before.

"Bad business, that."

Neil turned round. A man had come through a door and was reading the plaque with him. It was the big fair man who'd been in the café last night.

"Terrible night that was." He shook his head. "Hurricane force winds, sea rearing up, gusts up to 60, 80, 90 miles an hour –"

"What happened?"

"Well, they'd already rescued three off a ship. At the last minute they saw two more on the deck, waving frantically. The ship was sinking round them. So they turned round and went back. And a giant wave just took their boat, turned it over and smashed it down on the deck. The whole lot was lost. All lost." He sighed. "You don't get many storms like that, and lifeboats can right themselves and all sorts these days. But you can't ever trust the sea. Never."

Neil looked at the plaque again. The names of the dead crew were listed on it. He pointed to a name: T. Boswell.

"Was he – ?"

"That was my dad," said the man. "Tommy Boswell. I was seventeen then, and I joined the lifeboat crew the next day, to help start a new boat off again. And I've been in it ever since." He looked at Neil. "Know about lifeboats, do you?"

"No," said Neil. "I only came down here yesterday from London. I'm staying with my Aunt Tessa."

The man looked at him.

"At The Hermit Shell?"

"Yes."

"Tess never said you were coming."

"I – I only decided to come yesterday morning."

"Did you now?" The man's shaggy eyebrows went up. Then he grinned at Neil.

"Sounds the sort of thing she'd do herself," he said. "You must take after her."

He put out a large hand. "Mat Boswell."

"Neil Loftus." They shook hands.

"Tess feeding you all right?" Mat asked.

"Oh, yes," said Neil, although actually Tessa had hardly fed him at all this morning, and last night's supper had been nothing but pasta and grated cheese.

"She forgets," said Mat. "Once she starts painting she forgets all about food. Artists are like that sometimes. Look, Annis and I are just going over to Penna's Café for breakfast. Why don't you join us?"

"Well –"

"Can't have you going hungry," said Mat. "Come on."

4

The three of them walked round the harbour to the café.

Mat pushed the door open. Heat flooded out to them, and pounding music.

"Wayne?"

Mat raised his voice.

"Wake up, Wayne, my son. Brought you some

customers. Get the kettle on. And turn that racket off."

A tall thin young man with black hair in a pony tail was up a step-ladder behind the counter, hammering. He was wearing torn jeans and a T-shirt with 'Download the Surf' scrawled across the front. He climbed down, grinning at Mat and Annis, and turned down the radio.

"That's better. Hear yourself speak now," said Mat. "This is Wayne Penna, Neil. Neil's just come down from London, so he wants a bit of peace and quiet."

"No, I like the music," protested Neil.

"Good man," said Wayne approvingly.

Mat shook his head. "You youngsters. What about a spot of breakfast, Wayne?"

"On-line now." Wayne went to the coffee machine and set it whirring. "I'm getting the DIY bit done while I can. I'll be too busy in the summer. Sit down."

They sat at a table while Wayne cooked. Neil looked round at the fishing nets hanging from the ceiling, the walls covered in murals of humpbacked whales and surfers riding huge waves. There were stands with things to buy: cakes and paperbacks; teapots and ice-cream and scuba diving stuff. All sorts of things.

"You guys want any extras with it?" called Wayne. "Bit of fried bread?"

Neil's mouth watered. "Well . . ."

Wayne brought the plates and they ate, while he cooked again for three men who'd just come in from a night's fishing. Neil listened to them.

"Wind's dropped this morning."

"Yes, she's settling down a bit now."

Through the window, Neil saw that the tide was falling, leaving some of the boats in the harbour stranded on their sides in the mud.

"You must take Neil out in *Gannet* while he's here, Annis," said Mat, reaching for the marmalade. "That's *Gannet*, Neil, across there." He pointed to a small red and white rowing boat, upside down by the harbour railings. "Annis's pride and joy, that boat."

Neil looked at Annis enviously. It would be great to have your own boat, to take it wherever you wanted to go.

"How long are you down here for, Neil?" asked Annis.

"I don't know."

He put down his fork, suddenly not hungry any more. He'd forgotten all about Mum and Dad coming this afternoon to take him back to London.

The church clock was striking eleven as Tessa came round the harbour. She saw Annis out in *Gannet*, rowing slowly across the narrow stretch of open water near the harbour mouth, and Neil sitting on the slipway, watching her.

"Hello, Neil."

"Hello."

She gave him a quick look.

"All right?"

"Yes."

"That's good," she said. "Let's go shopping. We must get something nice for your mum and dad to eat when they come this afternoon."

They went up the hill to the shop that he'd seen from the bus.

"Now," said Tessa, looking round the shelves. "What?"

"I don't know," said Neil helplessly. He couldn't imagine Mum and Dad down here in Cornwall at all. It felt completely unreal.

In the end, Tessa chose everything and they came out, carrying a bag each.

"Want to try a Cornish pasty for lunch?" she suggested.

"No, I'm not hungry."

She stood still.

"Neil," she said. "If you want to tell me anything . . . If I can help at all . . ."

He shook his head and didn't answer. After a minute she put out a hand and squeezed his arm comfortingly. They walked back to The Hermit Shell in silence.

5

His parents came at half-past two.

Neil was standing at the window when his dad's taxi drew up. It blocked the light and made the whole room dark. His mother was in the front seat. She saw him at the window and gave him a quick embarrassed smile. He backed away quickly.

"I'll go," said Tessa as the knock came. "They can't leave the car there."

Neil went into the kitchen and shut the door. He stood by the draining board, fiddling with a spoon, listening to them talking on the doorstep. Tessa was saying something about a place to park the car.

"OK," he heard his father say. "I just hope I'll find my way back."

The car drove off and he heard Tessa and his mother come in and shut the door. Tessa came into the kitchen.

"Neil? Your mother's here."

He followed her out of the room slowly.

"Hello, Mum."

"Oh, Neil."

She came and gave him a hug, but she felt stiff and awkward and so did he.

"I'll make some tea," said Tessa. "Why don't you two sit down?"

She carried his mother's coat away, and vanished into the kitchen.

"Mum, I –" said Neil.

"Yes, well," said his mother. "It was a dreadful shock, Neil. Your dad rang to see where you were . . . then I found out you'd never been to school all day. It's just not like you. You've never done it before. You'd seemed perfectly all right in the morning. You were, weren't you?"

Neil shifted his feet. "Yes."

"Why didn't you tell us if you were worried about something? When Tessa rang and we found out you'd come all this way on your own . . ." She shook her head. "Such a long way. It's taken us hours to get here. Neil, why on earth did you – ?"

She stopped. Neil's father had come back and Tessa was coming in with the tea. They all sat down.

"Quiet sort of place," said his father, looking out of the window. "Brightens up in the summer, I suppose."

"Too many visitors then," said Tessa, passing some cake to him. "I like it in winter."

"Really?" he said. "What do you do in the evenings when it's dark? I mean, in London . . . Nothing here but watching the telly, is there?"

"I don't have a television."

"Good grief."

His parents looked wrong here, thought Neil, too big for the room, ill at ease.

Tessa didn't look very comfortable either. She was showing Neil's mother round now, taking her up to the studio.

Left alone, he and Dad stood around in the kitchen. Dad lit a cigarette, looked at the view, and then stubbed the cigarette out again.

"I wish you . . ." He started again. "Neil, Tessa told me on the phone she thought you were unhappy about something. Now, if that's true, why didn't you tell me when you saw me yesterday morning? Couldn't you have done that? What was it, bit of bother at school?"

Neil mumbled something.

"What?"

"Not only at school," said Neil. "At home, too."

His father frowned.

"What's the matter at home? I mean . . . Your mother and I have tried to make it all right for you. I come round as often as I can. It's much the same as when I was there all the time, isn't it?"

"No, it's –" Neil felt stunned. How could Dad think that? It was totally different. Totally.

"Neil?" Dad looked at him hopefully. "I come to see you, don't I? And Mum's always glad of my help. Most of the residents have known me for a long time, you see. They like me. I can do some of the heavy work, I ... " He spread his hands, asking for Neil's sympathy. "I only want to help."

Then why don't you stay away? Neil thought. But he didn't say it because Tessa and Mum were coming down again.

"Nice little house," said Mum. She looked at her watch. "Jim, we should go. I promised Carol I wouldn't be late. She isn't used to being in charge." She turned to Tessa. "I'm just sorry Neil should have landed himself on you like this."

"Yes, sorry about that, Tessa," said Dad. "All set, Neil? Ready to go?"

Neil's heart was thumping. He swallowed.

"I want to stay," he said. "I don't want to go back with you, I want to stay here."

There was a silence that went on and on.

"Now don't be silly ... " began his mother at last.

"Come along, son," said his father. "School on Monday."

"There's a room up in the roof," said Neil. "I've seen it from the beach. It looks right out over the sea."

"That's just the loft," said Tessa. She was looking at Neil rather hard. "It's full of my junk. It's tiny. It's dusty ..."

"I don't care."

"Neil," she said, "you'd be bored in a week and want to go back to London."

55

"I wouldn't." He was trembling. "This is the place I want to live."

He saw the three adults exchange glances.

"Sorry about all this," Dad said to Tessa. "I suppose it's the new school and the divorce and everything. We'll soon sort things out once he's home again. Running away's not the answer."

"It never is," said Mum. "As soon as we get home, Neil, we'll have a good talk, and I'll go and have a chat to your teachers –"

"No," said Neil. He was holding on tightly to the edge of the table. "I need to live here. I knew it as soon as I saw the crab on the fax. I need to live here. I need . . . "

Tears were rolling down his face. Mum tried to put her arms round him but he broke away and flung himself across the room. He wrenched open the front door and just ran.

6

He was nearly down to the harbour when Tessa caught him up.

He leaned on the wall, panting. He had to stay. He had to stay in The Hermit Shell and keep the entrance shut with his claw.

She didn't try to touch him, just stood beside him, staring out at the darkening sea.

"Tell me," she said at last. "Tell me what it's about."

He told her, not keeping anything back. He told her

about Mum and Dad, about school, about Martyn and Lee and the name-calling. All of it.

"I know all about needing to get away," said Tessa slowly. "I tried to do it by moving around all the time. But now I think what suits me is staying still."

Neil said nothing. He waited to see what she would say next.

"And does it have to be here?" she asked. They were walking slowly back up Ship Street by now.

"Yes," he said. "Sorry."

She sighed. "I'm sorry too. It was *my* house, *my* hermit shell. I've lived all over the place, with this person and that person, and now I want to be on my own. I like being on my own. I've told Mat, I –" She broke off.

"I could go to school here," he said. "People change schools all the time." A new school, he thought, a new start.

"It wouldn't be easy for either of us," she said. "I don't know anything about boys, and I'm not used to looking after anyone but myself. Just doing my own thing in my own way. If you did come ... "

His heart leapt.

"Yes?"

"We'd have to agree how to do it." They were standing outside the house now. "Have a rota of jobs or something. I haven't got time to look after you."

"I can look after myself."

She looked at him. "You're absolutely sure you want to come?"

He nodded.

"All right," she said, and pushed the door open. "We'll see what we can do."

After two hours, first with Tessa talking with his parents on their own, and then with everyone together, they'd hammered out an arrangement.

Neil could stay for one week. Then Dad would come down again, bringing some of Neil's clothes and belongings in the car. At that point Neil would choose. He could go back to London, return to school, and go on with his life as before. Or he could stay at The Hermit Shell and his dad would arrange for him to go to a local school. There was a lot of talk about school and money, about his parents paying for his keep. Once a month Neil would go home for the weekend, and in six months or so they would all review the situation.

It was settled. Or as settled as it could be.

By the end, everyone was tired out. Neil stood at the door to say goodbye.

"Neil, you are sure, aren't you?" his mother said anxiously as she kissed him. "Sure you want to stay here?"

"Yes, Mum."

He saw how his father's shoulders slumped.

"Remember," he came back to say, jingling his car keys in his pocket. "You've only got to pick up the phone, Neil. Day or night, doesn't matter. I'll come down and fetch you."

"Thanks, Dad."

His father looked mournfully along the dark, narrow street. It was drizzly now, and cold.

"Beats me," he said. He lowered his voice. "I don't think you'll find Tessa easy. I never did. Still, if it's what you want –"

"I'll be all right, Dad."

"Well –" He hugged him and slapped him on the back a few times. "I'll phone in a day or two. Oh, and I nearly forgot." He reached under his coat and fished out a roll of paper. "From Miss Cobham."

He hurried off to catch up with Neil's mother. Neil thought he heard her say something about his being home within a week. Then they turned the corner and were gone.

Slowly, he shut the door. Tessa was in the kitchen, washing dishes. He unrolled the paper and spread it on the table.

It was the poster from Miss Cobham's room, the one with the ocean liner and the big golden moon. 'SAIL THE WORLD WITH THE RANGOLD LINE,' it said. 'WE MAKE ALL YOUR DREAMS COME TRUE.'

Across one corner, Miss Cobham had pencilled, 'Give my love to Cornwall, and to yourself. Happy sailing. Primrose C.'

He rolled it up again. Would his dreams come true here?

He went into the kitchen. Tessa was at the sink. She gave him a small smile over her shoulder and he smiled back. In silence, he picked up a tea towel and began drying the cups.

What have I done? thought Tessa. What have I done?

CHAPTER FOUR

Friends

It was six weeks later. Neil was coming out of school.

The last bell of the day had just rung and pupils were streaming out into the early March sunshine, making for the waiting lines of cars and buses, unlocking their bicycles from the stands.

"Hey, Lofty!"

Danny Rapson kicked a stone and sent it spinning in Neil's direction. Neil caught it on the edge of his foot, twisted round and flicked it back. Danny returned it.

"Nice one." Pete Maddaford ran backwards, cannoning into a group of girls as he flapped his hands in encouragement. "Over here, Lofty, over here!"

"That's enough of that, you boys." A passing teacher put

out her arm and swung Pete round the right way. "No kicking about on the drive. You'll hurt someone in a minute."

"Sorry, Miss," muttered Pete. Danny winked at Neil. Craig Cowling, who was rather fat, spluttered with laughter.

"Anyway, Neil, how's it going?" the teacher asked, dropping into step with him. "Settling down here?"

"Yes, thanks," said Neil. He looked across the green playing fields and took a big breath of the fresh, clear air that blew in from the sea. "It's like I've been here for years."

It was true. He felt at home at this school, had done ever since he started, even from the day he and his father had come to look round and see if there was a place for him. He just seemed to fit in right away. He was coping with the work better than he'd dared hope. Perhaps it was because he'd covered some of it already at his other school. Perhaps it was because the teachers understood he was new and gave him extra help. Or perhaps it was because he had friends now, and was happy.

He could still hardly believe it. Danny and Pete and Craig were his friends. That first day, when he'd been so nervous, most people had been friendly. But these three had really singled him out, they'd made a point of coming over to talk to him, to include him, and his nervousness had melted away. Within a week he was one of them, one of the gang, Danny and Pete and Craig and Lofty. Nowadays the four of them sat together in class, they hung around together at lunch time, they did everything together. It was absolutely different from his last school. It was great.

They'd reached the bike stands. Neil waited while the others collected their bicycles, then they all walked on down the drive to Neil's bus stop.

"Here Lofty, where's Annis Boswell today?"

Neil shrugged. "She wasn't on the bus this morning. Maybe she's ill."

"She your girlfriend, Lofty?"

Neil blushed. "No."

"I think we'd better go out to Portmartin tonight. See what they get up to in the evenings. Cheers, Lofty."

"See you, Lofty."

"See you."

They wheeled off down the road, swerving and shoving and shouting. Neil stood at the bus stop, smiling. 'Lofty' wasn't such a bad nickname. It made him feel taller, older. It was much better than that other name, that London one. It was good to have mates.

2

The bus pulled in by Portmartin harbour.

"Thanks," Neil called to the driver, and headed off round the harbour towards the sea. Even now, after several weeks, it gave him a bit of a thrill each time.

I live here, he thought, breathing in the familiar salty air, hearing the cries of gulls circling the boats. I actually live here.

For that was how it was now. As arranged, his father

had come down from London again after Neil's first week at The Hermit Shell. But by then there had not been much question about it. For the time being, Neil was going to live in Portmartin and go to school each day on the bus.

The arrangements had taken a day or two. When his father left to go back to London alone, Neil could see he was disappointed. Perhaps, though, thought Neil, watching him, he was secretly relieved too. Perhaps Neil hadn't been the only one who'd needed a breathing space.

For Neil, it was all turning out to be a great success. Even his first weekend at home hadn't changed his mind. On the contrary, everything in London had felt unreal, as if he no longer fitted in there. All he'd wanted to do was talk about Cornwall, but nobody had time to listen – not even Miss Cobham.

"Neil," she'd greeted him as he came out of his room. "So you went. That's right, that's right." She'd nodded her approval, looking up at him with her bright blue eyes. Then she'd hobbled away and their paths hadn't crossed again.

His mother had taken him shopping for new clothes, and he'd gone to the football with his father. And something funny had happened at the game. He'd met a boy, Steve, from his old school. Steve had mentioned the Norfolk holiday. And when Neil asked if Martyn and Lee were still going, Steve had looked blank. Martyn and Lee had never been on the list at all. So Martyn had tricked Neil on the train that morning, pretending that brown envelope had contained holiday money.

But all that seemed long ago and far away. None of it

mattered now. When Neil had finally left on the Sunday, weighed down with cakes and sweets from his mother, he'd felt nothing but relief. At the end of the journey lay The Hermit Shell and the sea.

Now he climbed Ship Street, whistling and swinging his school bag. His homework was no worry. He'd settle down to it later this evening, sitting round the fire with Tessa, perhaps, or up in his room. After all, what else was there to do in the evenings? There was no TV. But that was no problem. Not really.

Someone was walking behind him. He turned round.

"Hello, Neil."

"Oh, hi, Annis."

They went on up the street together.

"Did they show that video in History this morning?" she asked. "Have they set any homework on it?"

Neil explained the homework. "Were you ill today, then?" he asked.

"I'll be all right tomorrow." She stopped at the house with the yellow shutters. "Do you want to go out in the boat? The tide's right."

He glanced at the sky. "Will it be light long enough?"

"If we're quick changing," she said. "See you by *Gannet* in ten minutes."

He pushed his key in the door and raced up the stairs to the studio, pulling off his school tie. Then he saw Mat Boswell was there, talking to Tessa as she painted.

"So we had him on the stretcher all right," he was saying, "and the helicopter chaps started to winch him up . . . How are you, Neil? Had a good day?"

"Fine, thanks."

"That's good."

It was a bit awkward sometimes, having to cross Tessa's studio to get upstairs to his room at the top of the house.

"Mat and the lifeboat crew have been out today on a training exercise," said Tessa, scraping at a painting with a flat knife.

"We were doing cliff rescues just along the coast," said Mat. "Practising with the helicopter. Nice easy day compared with yesterday."

The day before, Portmartin lifeboat had been called to attend a fishing boat, stranded and rolling helplessly with a fouled propeller. The crew had been out there for hours before they towed it in successfully.

Neil went on up the stairs and shut his door, dropping his bag on the floor, scrambling about for his old jeans and jumper. Pulling them on, he looked round the room happily. He and Tessa had worked hard on it, stacking her cartons and suitcases at one end and sweeping away the cobwebs. They had arranged a folding bed for him, a rickety table and chair, and bought a couple of rugs. They'd put up a rail across one corner for his clothes. He didn't mind the cold or the musty smell or the low sloping ceiling. Miss Cobham's poster looked good on the plain white wall by his bed. And it was his, all his. There couldn't be another room like it in the country. Not with a view like that.

He never got tired of it. Looking out of that window he felt like a captain on the bridge of his ship, or a bird flying out over the sea. There was always something to watch: boats going in and out of the harbour, oil tankers passing along the horizon, huge black rain clouds travelling across the sky, the sun rising behind the headland. It was like a film unrolling, a film that never ended. It was always different. It was the best view in the world.

He checked the sea now. There was a gentle swell, nothing much, just enough to send white spray up on the rocks as the waves broke. Perhaps Annis would let him take *Gannet* beyond the harbour today.

He picked up his jacket and went down.

"Where are you going?" asked Tessa.

"Annis and I are taking *Gannet* out."

"Have you brought the logs in from the shed? It's going to be cold tonight." Neil had chosen looking after the fire as one of his jobs. He'd thought it would be fun, more fun than doing his own washing and ironing or helping with the shopping, which he also had to do.

"I'll do it when I come back," he said. "I've got to meet Annis first."

"Do the logs now," said Tessa. "Don't leave them to me. I've got to get my pictures ready for the show. You know it's hanging day tomorrow."

"I know that." How could he help knowing? Two dates had been ringed in red on the calendar for weeks now: tomorrow, the day when Tessa's pictures would be hung up for her exhibition, and the day after, when the exhibition opened. Yet still her pictures didn't seem to be ready.

"I won't be able to stop to do your jobs for you," she

66

said. "I need every minute of daylight."

"So do I," he argued. "For going out in the boat."

Mat looked from one to the other, saying nothing.

"Look, Neil," said Tessa, "get those logs in now as you go. And be back before dark, OK?"

"OK," said Neil, "OK." He wished Tessa wouldn't keep on at him.

He went downstairs. For a moment, he paused on the doorstep. Then he slammed the door and raced off down Ship Street towards the harbour.

3

It was very cold in the boat. Even the oars were cold. Neil ducked his head and blew on his purple hands. He wished he had some gloves.

"Careful," said Annis, sitting in the stern. "Look where you're going."

Neil gave a hasty glance over his shoulder, saw that *Gannet* was about to hit a buoy, and pulled on his right oar once or twice to get the boat straight again.

"That's enough. Not too much."

"I wasn't."

"All right."

He took a firmer grip on his oars and concentrated on rowing absolutely evenly, just to show Annis he could do it. She'd been teaching him to row for weeks now and he reckoned he was nearly as good as she was.

"It's all cluttered up with boats in here," he said. "Why

can't we go out of the harbour?"

"You're not ready for that yet," said Annis. "There are rocks out there and currents that can sweep you away. Or a storm could blow up. You don't realise."

Neil looked up at the misty evening sky. The light was fading fast and a pale moon was just rising behind the hill.

"What storm?" he said. "It's boring, going round and round the harbour."

"It isn't."

"Like learning to run in a car park full of cars."

"That's silly. Go round once more and then we'll stop."

He glowered at her and obeyed, dipping the oars in carelessly now, making *Gannet* rock from side to side. He saw she was holding on to the sides of the boat, but she didn't say anything.

"You were wearing uniform," he said suddenly.

"What?" She looked up. "When?"

"Just now, when we walked up Ship Street. You were wearing school uniform. But you haven't been to school today."

"I know," said Annis. "I put on my uniform this morning because I thought I was going."

"Then you felt ill and didn't go."

"Yes."

He held the oars out of the water and watched the water drip from them.

"Your dad thinks you went," he said.

"What?"

"I've just seen your dad. I said we were taking *Gannet*

out and he didn't say anything about you being ill. He wouldn't like you going out in *Gannet* if you were ill. And I remember now, I saw him wave you off this morning."

"No, he –"

"When I was going down for the bus, I looked back and saw you come out of your house carrying your school bag, waving to your dad. But when I got to the bus I looked back again and you'd disappeared."

"I felt ill suddenly," she said. "I went back home."

"Did you?" He stared at her and her eyes dropped. "Your dad would have known about it, he'd have said something about it just now. Where did you go all day? Why did you turn up just as I got off the bus? You still had your uniform on. You were pretending you'd been to school, weren't you?"

"I told you, I –"

"You've done it before." Suddenly it all made sense to him. "Haven't you? Pretended to go to school and then not gone? You did it last week, pretending to catch the bus in the morning and then pretending to get off it in the afternoon. Are you going to take an absence note to school tomorrow, like you did then? A note from your dad?"

"Shut up." She stood up, setting *Gannet* bucking and tilting in the water. "Move over. I'll take the boat in."

He clung on, afraid of capsizing.

"Look," he said. "I didn't mean –"

"I said shut up."

In silence they changed places. He looked at Annis's set face as she rowed, seeing how pale she was. He shouldn't have said all that. Perhaps he was wrong. Perhaps she really had suddenly felt ill. Annis was clever at school, popular with everyone. She wasn't the sort of person who would ever truant.

They reached the slipway and Annis edged the boat close. Neil jumped ashore.

"Annis, I'm sorry, I –"

"Take your lifejacket off," she said, not looking at him. As he peeled it off, he heard a laugh above him. He looked up and saw Pete and Craig leaning over the rails, and Danny alongside, all of them astride their bikes.

"Hi ya, Lofty. Hi ya, Annis. That your boat?"

"Yes."

"Nice."

Neil could feel their eyes on him all the time as, clumsily, he helped Annis drag the boat up the slipway and turn it over.

"We've come to see what Portmartin's like," said Danny. "Show us round, Annis."

Annis shook her head, chaining the boat to the railings and snapping the padlock shut. "I'm going home to have my tea."

"That's a shame." He grinned round at the others. "Lofty, then. You'll come with us."

Neil hesitated, looking at Annis. She looked away.

"OK."

He climbed on the back of Danny's bike, and the four of them spun away round the darkening village, laughing, leaving Annis standing there alone.

4

It was good fun being out in the village with his mates. Neil thought he'd had enough females telling him what to do for a while.

The streets of Portmartin were steep and, with two people on a bike, you could come down a hill at top speed. Neil clung on to Danny, his legs straight out on either side for balance, screaming like the others.

"Yaaaaah!" They shot down Fore Street, round the square and down to the harbour again, skimming round it at the very edge of the water, shouting and laughing. Then Pete, in the lead, thudded over a coil of rope and they all landed in a heap on top of him.

"Good run, that."

"Do it again?"

"Give Lofty your bike, Craig. You can run and get some of that fat off."

"No way."

They rolled on the ground, kicking and pushing. Then they dusted themselves down and picked up the bikes.

"Where now?"

"Across there."

They wheeled the bikes over the road and into a little garden with railings round it. They flopped down in a row on a seat. Danny took cans of drinks and some chocolate out of his bag and shared them out. Then he leaned back and stared all around.

"This is a boring place you live in, Lofty," he said. "It's better in town. Or London. You'd have been better staying in London, Lofty."

"I wouldn't," said Neil. "It isn't boring here, it's . . . " But he couldn't explain to them how he felt about Portmartin.

"Nothing to do here," said Danny. "It's a real dump." He drained his can and screwed up his chocolate wrapper. Pete got up and began swinging by his arms from one of the trees.

"Come on, you lot," he called. "See who can go the highest."

They all swung from branches. Then Danny dropped to the ground and ran over to Pete.

"Two at a time," he shouted. "Try two at a time." He sprang up and grabbed Pete round the middle.

Craa-aa-ack . . .

The branch broke. Danny and Pete tumbled to the ground, yelling.

"My foot!"

"Get off me, Pete, get off."

They climbed to their feet and looked down at the broken branch. Danny dragged it along the ground a little way and then left it.

"Too heavy," he said. "Let's go."

The three boys, Pete limping, collected their bikes and climbed on.

"See you tomorrow, Lofty."

"See you."

They rattled away down the street and their voices faded into the dark.

Neil looked round him. The grass around the seat was

littered with cans and wrappers. He bent down and started picking them up.

"Hi, Neil."

He looked up. Wayne Penna was on the path, staring up at the damaged tree.

"Hi, Wayne." He showed him the litter he was collecting. "I'm just clearing this up."

"Right," said Wayne. "Dirty rats, some people. You'd think they'd have more respect. And look at that tree. It's never going to look right again." He shook his head. "That's Tommy Boswell's tree, that one."

Neil pushed his handful of litter in the nearest bin and came back.

"Mat's dad?"

"Yep." Wayne pointed at a little plaque down by the trunk. It had Tommy Boswell's name on it. "Seen the others, have you?"

"No."

"Eight trees planted here for eight men lost. A name on every one."

"Oh." Neil looked around, counting the trees. "So what is this place?" he asked.

"Nobody told you that?" Wayne seemed surprised. "It's the Memorial Garden, for the men lost on the lifeboat years ago."

He pointed to each tree in turn, giving each man's name as if he had been a friend of his, though he couldn't have been born when the disaster happened.

" . . . Joe Tregannis, young Andy Wilmer," he finished, "and that's the tree for my uncle, Richard Penna.

Come on. Let's go."

They walked to the gate.

"A gate won't keep vandals out," said Wayne. "But we don't have a lot of vandals in Portmartin. It was nice of you to clear up like that. Shame you didn't see who did it."

"Yes. Yes, it is."

They shut the gate. Wayne looked down at Neil.

"All of us in Portmartin," he said, "we think a lot of those eight men. When they died, people knew they couldn't bring them back, but at least they could make a garden so anyone could come in to sit quiet and have a bit of a rest. And I guess that's what those eight would like if you could ask them."

5

When Neil got back to The Hermit Shell, all the lights were on. The fire was lit and the log basket was full.

"Hello," he called. "I'm back."

Tessa came running down the stairs.

"Oh, thank goodness, Neil. Whatever happened to you? Where have you been?"

"Out in the boat. Then just sort of messing around."

"Messing around? Do you know what time it is?" She followed him up to the studio. "I came back from the gallery nearly an hour ago. I couldn't believe you weren't back. I thought something must have happened. I've been really scared, Neil."

"Sorry," he said. He started climbing the stairs to his

room. She went on following him.

"Sorry's not good enough. I told you to be back by dark. And what about the logs?"

"You've done them," he said.

"Not me. Mat brought them in before he left."

"OK, then." He opened his door.

"It isn't OK. You're supposed to do jobs round the house. I've got the show opening tomorrow. I've been working day and night, and then you just go out and stay out. And look at this room."

He jerked his head up. "What's wrong with it?"

"Wrong with it?" She laughed shortly. "Just look at it, Neil. Clothes dropped where you took them off, the bed not made, your books and tapes all over the place . . . You've turned this room into an absolute tip."

"I haven't."

"Just at the moment, Neil," she said, "I wish you'd never come here."

"Don't nag me," he cried. "You're worse than –" Worse than my mum, he'd been going to say, but Tessa had slammed the door and run downstairs.

Slowly, he started picking up clothes and hanging them on the rail. The room wasn't a tip, it was beautiful, it was his, his to do what he liked with. Tessa had no right to come in and tell him what to do.

He stood at the window, listening to the sea splashing in the blackness outside, thinking of the evening ahead. Just him and Tessa in the house, no television, and a bagful of homework to get through.

Without warning, a wave of homesickness filled his

chest, homesickness for the warmth and lights and bustle of the Quiet Corner Rest Home. He wrapped his arms round himself and shivered.

CHAPTER FIVE

Hanging Day

When Neil came down next morning, Tessa was already on the phone talking about her pictures.

"Look, it's hanging day," she kept saying. "Hanging day. Those pictures have to be put on those gallery walls today, ready for the show to open tomorrow morning. What chance is there of that at the moment? None. None whatsoever."

Silently, Neil went into the kitchen and got himself some bread and marmalade. He stood eating it, twiddling knobs on the radio and staring out at the sea.

"Neil!" she called from the living room. "That radio, do you mind? I'm trying to talk."

"That's why I've got it on," he muttered, but he turned it

down. In the garden two gulls were squabbling over a piece of bread they must have taken from someone's bird-table.

Tessa came into the kitchen.

"I wish I'd never thought of this wretched show." She switched the radio off, sat down and then got up again and made herself some black coffee.

"I still can't make up my mind which pictures to put in," she said. She pushed her hair back. "There's one upstairs I don't know if it's good enough . . . I'll fetch it. See what you think."

"Don't bother," he felt like saying, but she'd gone flying upstairs.

She came down again with a picture and propped it up on the draining board.

"What do you think?" she asked.

It was a swirl of blue and green splodges. He had no idea what it was meant to be. He shrugged.

"I don't know."

"Oh, come on," she said. "You could show a bit more interest than that. You must have an opinion of some kind."

"Not really."

"For goodness sake, Neil," she exploded. "What's the matter with you?"

"Nothing. It's time to go. I'll be late."

"Go on, then. Don't hang round here. You're all right, aren't you?"

She drained her coffee cup and went back to study the picture moodily. "Trouble is, if I change a picture I'll have to alter all the catalogues by hand. Why on earth did I have so many printed? Nobody's going to come, I'm quite sure of –"

"Oh, stop moaning!" he said and slammed the door as hard as he could.

Tessa blinked and shook her head.

"Neil," she called, but he'd gone.

She went on sitting at the kitchen table, looking blankly at the dirty dishes and the crumbs. Perhaps just lately she had let her show take up too much of her time. But it was so important.

Sighing, she pushed Neil to the back of her mind and reached for her picture, turning it to the light, trying to decide once and for all if it really was any good.

2

Running down Ship Street to the bus, Neil wished people wouldn't ask you if you were all right if they didn't even wait for an answer. His homework wasn't all right for one thing. He'd got in a total mess with the maths last night and in the end he'd put it away unfinished. Tessa hadn't noticed. She never took any interest in his homework because her head was full of all that wretched painting.

He arrived at the bus stop just in time to see Annis climbing on the bus. At registration time at school he watched her hand in an absence note for the previous day. As the tutor read it Neil studied his face. But he made no comment, just gave a smile to Annis and put the note away in a folder.

The day passed slowly. As he'd expected, the maths lesson at the end of the afternoon went badly. He couldn't follow what the teacher was saying and after a time he gave up trying. When he'd started at this school the work had all seemed easy. Now it didn't. That was the trouble with school: as soon as you understood something, they were off onto something harder, and then harder again, until you were totally lost.

He and Danny sat in the corner with their maths books open on the table, secretly drawing on their wrists with felt-tip pens. Danny drew an alien hanging from a lamp post. Neil drew a hermit crab in a very small spiral shell, with one of its claws barring the entrance. He was just adding another hermit crab outside, looking at it, when the teacher leaned over his shoulder.

"Come on, Neil, you've hardly started this work yet."

Neil pulled down his shirt sleeve. "I'm just going to do some more."

"Hurry up then." He moved on.

Neil sat hunched over his book. He could have said he didn't understand what he had to do. But then Danny and the others would laugh at him, show him up. It was better just to muddle along as he was and hope to catch up another time. He reached for a felt-tip pen again.

"What you doing after school, Danny?" he asked, extending the claws of the two crabs.

"Nothing much."

"Come out to Portmartin again," said Neil. "You and

the rest, like yesterday. We'll have a bit of a laugh."

He put in one last touch of the pen and the crabs' claws met and locked together, fighting.

3

He was down on the beach when they came.

He knew they were coming because the bus had passed them on the road not long after leaving the school. Danny and Pete and Craig, bent double over their handlebars, had been cycling flat out, racing the bus, then waving and gesturing to Neil as it roared past them.

He had walked home to The Hermit Shell but, as he'd expected, it was cold and empty. No doubt Tessa was still doing her hanging. He thought about it as he made himself some tea and rummaged for biscuits, laughing a bit at the thought of Tessa busy with noose and gallows. Then he wandered outside, climbed the garden wall and sat on the rocks, hugging his mug. The sea lapped around him.

It was so quiet here. Too quiet. He shut his eyes and concentrated hard. The sounds came back, the London sounds he'd been born to. The high-pitched whine of an underground train; the roar of traffic in the streets; the babble of the huge television set in the residents' lounge. The television was always turned up loud, and usually had a circle of elderly people round it. When he came home from school they'd look up – well, some of them would – and say hello and ask him how he was. Then Mum would come in with the big tea trolley. Sometimes someone would pass a box of chocolates round. There always seemed to be chocolates, and someone to chat to, and the television was always on. He missed that. And he missed the talks he used to have with Miss Cobham . . .

"Ow!"

He ducked. A pebble had hit the back of his head. Another one struck his shoulder. He turned round. Danny and Pete and Craig were leaning over the garden wall, laughing at him.

"This your home, Lofty?"

"This where you live with your auntie?"

He waved to them. "Leave your bikes there. Come down here."

They sat together on the rocks and threw pebbles into the sea.

"Ducks and Drakes," said Danny, flicking a pebble sideways to make it bounce along the surface, "like this." But only Craig could do it properly. Then they walked along the beach with their hands in their pockets, kicking up the sand.

"I ought to go home," said Craig, looking at his watch. "My mum doesn't know I came out here."

"Chicken," jeered Danny. "I can stay out as long as I like, can't you, Pete?"

"And me," said Neil. "My auntie doesn't care what I do." It sounded funny to call Tessa that; he knew she didn't like it.

They went up the harbour steps and wandered round for a while. Danny and Pete had a pocketful of pebbles each. They kept shying them at boats and then pretending they hadn't. One hit a small cabin cruiser and chipped a bit of its paintwork.

"Wasn't me," said Danny, wide-eyed with innocence. "It was Pete."

"Wasn't."

"Was."

They pushed each other and staggered into a pile of lobster cages. Two cages fell into the water. A fisherman working on one of the boats shouted something and they all ran round to the other side of the harbour.

"In here," called Pete, swerving in through the open doors of the lifeboat house. The others followed.

"What's this, then?" said Danny, staring up at *Dolly Hescomb* standing high and silent on her carriage.

"The lifeboat," said Neil.

"I know that, fishface. I'm Cornish, aren't I? Not like you, Londoner. I know about lifeboats." Danny started walking round the boat, tapping at its navy-blue sides.

"Up here," he called, starting up the steps of the viewing platform. "Let's get on board."

"We shouldn't . . ." Neil began, looking round for Mat. But Mat must have gone home for tea with Annis; he'd left the boat house open for visitors to call in, knowing nothing would come to harm.

"Shouldn't what?" Pete and Danny were up on the platform now, climbing over the guide rails, standing on the deck.

"Don't," said Neil. Danny rattled at the heavy watertight door of the orange wheelhouse.

"Let's get in here and drive it off."

"That's stupid," said Craig.

"Don't, don't," implored Neil, at the foot of the steps. "Come down."

"It's locked anyway." Danny jumped off the steps. "Shame, that. I fancied taking her out, didn't you, Pete?"

They ran down to the far end of the boat house.

"Hey, Pete, look at these."

"No, don't –" But Neil was too late to stop them. Danny and Pete had found the crew's boots, waders and protective clothing and were pulling them down, trying them on.

"Look, look." Danny was strutting round in boots much too big for him, while Pete was attempting to pull on huge yellow waterproof trousers. "Don't we look like –"

"Hey!"

Neil spun round. Wayne Penna was standing in the doorway.

"Who told you kids you could mess around in here?" he demanded.

"Nobody. I –"

"How dare you touch that stuff!"

"Come on, Pete." Neil was nearly pushed over as Pete and Danny, strewing clothes behind them, shoved past him and fled outside.

"Come on, Lofty, *come on*." Craig seized his arm.

"You young devils," yelled Wayne, "come back here!"

Craig and Neil raced down the road behind Danny and Pete. As they skidded round the corner, Neil could hear Wayne's feet pounding along just behind him.

Wayne was gaining on them. Neil's breath was gasping in his chest and he had a stitch in his side. He stumbled on the rough ground, recovered himself and ran on.

"Can't catch us!" Danny yelled from in front, jumping on the upturned *Gannet* and waving his arms in triumph. Pete was trying to pull down a lifebelt that was fixed to the wall behind him. Danny helped him. Together, they wrenched it off its fastenings and hurled it as hard as they could into the harbour.

"Can't catch us! Can't catch us!"

"Oh, can't I?" Wayne made a grab. "You FOOLS. What d'you think you're doing?"

He grabbed again but it was only Neil he caught. Danny and Pete and Craig were already racing up Ship Street.

"Somebody's going to be down in the water one day," Wayne shouted after them, "screaming for help. And there won't be a lifebelt to chuck to them because you idiots have thrown it away. Thought of that, have you?"

He turned back to Neil and shook him like a dog shakes a rat, his fingers digging into his shoulders. "You total, blithering FOOLS."

"I tried to stop them . . ." Frightened, Neil stared up at Wayne. "I . . ."

Slowly, Wayne let his hands drop. Neil stood still, rubbing his shoulders.

"You kids," Wayne said at last. "What gets into you?"

"It was just a bit of fun at first," said Neil. "Then we went in the lifeboat house and they started messing round."

"Who's *they*?" demanded Wayne. "I want their names, Neil."

"What?"

"I'm stopping this before it gets any worse. Someone could die because of what you lot have done. Tell me their names."

Neil backed away, shaking his head. "They'd kill me."

"Tough."

"I can't grass on them."

Wayne made a disgusted face.

"Come on, Neil. Don't give me that stuff. You know who they are. At your school, are they? In your class? Thought so. Tell me the names. Tomorrow I'll phone the school and –"

Beep . . . Beep . . . Beep . . . Beep . . . Beep . . .

Startled, Neil stared at Wayne. He saw him take a small electronic gadget from his pocket.

"What is it?"

"My pager," said Wayne. "A shout's just gone off for the lifeboat crew. I've got to go."

"I never knew you were in the lifeboat crew," said Neil. "You don't look as if you are."

"I never knew you were a vandal," retorted Wayne. "You don't look as if you are either. Now, tell me those names and for God's sake be quick about it."

They stared at each other for ten long seconds.

Then Neil told him the three names and Wayne scribbled them down.

"Craig wasn't so bad," Neil tried to say. "He only –"

But Wayne had already stuffed the notebook in his

pocket and was running towards the boat house, stripping off his jacket. He shouted something over his shoulder.

"What?" Neil ran to keep up.

"I said come with me," Wayne yelled. Then, as Neil hesitated, he added, "Do you good to come and watch. But get in the way and I'll throttle you. Now, come ON."

5

It was beginning to get dark but the lifeboat house blazed with light and bustled with activity.

"Out of the way, lad. Stand back."

Two crew members, sweeping up in a car, nearly knocked Neil off his feet as they flung open the car doors and raced into the boat house.

"Hello, Neil." Mat, pushing past, gave him a friendly grin. Neil avoided his eye and retreated outside. He held onto the harbour rails, watching.

The crew were milling round, pulling on their protective clothing and lifejackets. Neil saw that one of the crew was a woman.

"Where's my boot?" Someone was scrabbling under the boat where Danny and Pete had thrown things as they ran. "What the devil's it doing under there?"

With a roar, the launching tractor behind the boat revved up, preparing to push her out to the water. Mat climbed up on deck and called his crew in while another man noted down their names.

"Bill, good man. Come on, Trevor. No, not you, John,

not tonight, sorry. I'll take Paul. And Sue. Have you got that down? And where's Wayne? Ah, here he is. Get moving, lad, if you want to come with us. What have you been up to, powdering your nose?"

"Just coming, Cox." Wayne sprang up the steps, grinning, and Neil saw he had already forgotten all about him. "Coming as fast as I can. Not as young as I was."

With mock cheers the older men hauled Wayne aboard. Already the boat, mounted on her carriage, was starting to move, heading across the road for the slipway into the harbour. Neil stared up at it as it ground past him with the launchers walking alongside. It rolled down the slipway and on across the exposed, dry part of the harbour towards the edge of the water.

Standing with the rest of the crowd that had gathered to see them off, Neil strained in the fading light to see what was happening. He heard the boat's engines start up, saw her lights come on, saw the launchers busy with the carriage and the crew moving about on deck. Then she was tilting, sliding off the front of the carriage, and she was afloat. The next moment she was off, roaring away in the dusk towards the harbour mouth with Mat at the controls.

"Heard there's a yacht out there in trouble," said a man behind Neil. "Capsized. People in the water."

"The lifeboat'll need to be quick," someone said. "Once you're in the water you haven't got long. The cold gets you. You can't hang on no longer and you just let go."

Neil shivered, looking at the chilly grey of the open sea, growing darker and more lonely every moment. He tried to imagine being out in all that vastness, clinging onto an upturned boat.

"They'll find them," said the man. "What wonderful work, going out and saving lives like that."

"Stupid."

Neil turned round and saw Annis pushing her way out of the crowd. He ran after her.

"What's the matter?"

She was walking fast up Ship Street.

"Nothing," she said. "I just can't bear people talking like that sometimes."

He walked up with her, half running to keep up, not understanding what she had said. As they came near The Hermit Shell he saw lights on inside and Tessa in the doorway.

"Hello, Annis."

"Come in and wait for your dad," said Neil and she nodded. The lamp light fell on her face and he saw it was tight with misery.

6

That night, Neil couldn't sleep.

Every time he shut his eyes he could hear Wayne Penna saying, *"Their names, Neil. Tell me their names"*, and his own voice protesting that he couldn't grass on them.

And then he had.

He turned over restlessly. He could hear Tessa moving around in the studio below him, still worrying about her show, he supposed. He and Tessa had hardly exchanged a word after he'd come in from the lifeboat launch. He'd done his homework, or as much of it as he could manage, and while Tessa had been playing cards with Annis, he had pretended to read a book.

Just as Tessa was talking about it being time for them to go to bed, they'd heard Mat at the door. Tessa had got up to let him in.

"Was it all right?" she asked. "Did you get the people off the yacht?"

"We got them," Mat said. "Four of them clinging to the boat, nearly ready to give up."

"They must have been glad to see you," said Neil.

Mat nodded soberly.

"We were just in time. They were frozen near to death. They couldn't have held on much longer. The ambulance has taken them off to hospital for a check up, but they'll be all right." He shook his head. "Trouble is, some people have boats, don't really know how to handle them. It gets dark, the wind comes up and –"

"And you risk your lives," said Tessa.

Mat shrugged.

"All part of the job," he said. "Maybe they'll be a bit more careful next time. Come on, Annis. School in the morning. Thanks a lot, Tessa."

"No problem," Tessa said. She gave him a smile and a quick pat on the arm as they went.

Once he was in bed Neil kept thinking about the people clinging to the capsized boat, shivering with cold, their hands starting to slip as they waited and waited for help to come. He couldn't stop pictures of it coming into his mind. And every time he did manage to forget it, he started thinking about Wayne Penna again, and how he'd told him the names of his mates.

Tomorrow Wayne would phone the school and report what had happened. They'd all get into trouble. But much worse than that, Danny and Pete and Craig would know it was Neil who'd given them away, because who else in Portmartin would have known their names? They'd blame Neil, and he wouldn't be able to deny it. Neil would be a grasser, a squealer, an informer, an outcast.

He groaned out loud and felt the sweat break out all over his body. He pushed off the bedclothes, sat up and lifted the curtain behind his head. The moon shone, cool and pale and infinitely far away in the sky, throwing a silver shimmer on the dark water. He thought again about the people clinging on to the yacht, helpless and frightened, with nothing but the wide empty sea all around them.

And then he thought again of how he had to go to school tomorrow. In just a few hours he'd be there, facing Danny and Pete and Craig, knowing what he'd done to betray them.

CHAPTER SIX

Look-out Post

It was the very best sort of March morning.

A soft west wind was blowing up from Land's End, gusting across the cliffs around Portmartin, sending little white clouds scudding over the blue sky.

Neil, flat on his back on the grass beside the Coast Path, narrowed his eyes and squinted up at the sun. As long as it didn't rain he'd be all right. He pulled himself to a sitting position and looked at his watch. Half past ten.

He reached for his school bag, hunted through it and found the Mars bar he'd bought yesterday at school and then forgotten to eat. He bit into it, gazing out across the clear blue sea that thrashed restlessly a long way below him. The wind had whipped the sea up into white flecks.

He watched the waves breaking over a flat-topped rock, the water draining down from it each time like custard poured over a pudding.

He turned his head. A thin brown dog was trotting along the narrow path towards him. Behind it came a grey-haired woman in a purple and white jacket and brown trousers, helping herself along with a tall stick. She whistled to the dog and it stood still for a moment looking back, waiting for her, and then it ran ahead. She stopped and looked down at Neil, giving him a friendly smile.

"Hello."

The dog bustled back to see what was keeping her and began sniffing at Neil and at the crumbs of chocolate on his school jumper.

"That's enough, Tigs." The woman called the dog off. "Lovely up here today, isn't it? We seem to have it all to ourselves. You haven't seen any seals, have you?"

"What?"

"Seals," said the woman, pointing to the flat-topped rock. "Apparently you can sometimes see them swimming around down there, or basking on that rock. Have a look."

She took the binoculars from around her neck and offered them to Neil. He shook his head. He wished she'd go away.

"Go on," she said. "You might just be lucky, see their heads bobbing up in the water. My guide book says this is one of the best places on the whole Coast Path for spotting seals. It would make my holiday if I could see some."

He took the binoculars and held them to his eyes, seeing nothing but a grey fog.

"Thanks."

He handed them back and turned away from her, feeling her eyes on him. But when he glanced round she was staring out to sea, smiling a little. Then at last she stirred.

"Come on, then, Tigs. Say goodbye."

Tigs sniffed again at Neil.

"Bye," he said.

"Enjoy your day."

He sat still, watching her figure getting smaller as she trudged on up over the headland, the dog running and sniffing around in front. Eventually the path bent to the left and they went out of sight.

He got to his feet and shouldered his bag. It would be just as well to move on. He was still a bit too near Portmartin for comfort. Someone who knew him by sight might come along at any moment and ask him what he was up to.

2

He never really knew at what point he'd decided not to go to school. Perhaps it was at breakfast time. Tessa had been rushing round, a towel round her wet hair, opening Good Luck cards, making phone calls, and running up and down the stairs.

"You might take an interest, Neil," she'd said. "This is a big day for me. What's that you're reading?"

"A letter from Dad." It was all about the football match

Dad had been to last Saturday. Neil wished he'd been there. He really missed going to the football with Dad.

"Any message for me?" asked Tessa. He shook his head and went on reading.

"Typical Jim," said Tessa. "He's forgotten it's the show today. Oh well. Now come on, Neil, you'll be late."

He collected his books for school and the materials for his technology project, and then he began hunting for his PE kit. He finally found it in the kitchen, still mud-stained and in its bag, just as he'd left it there two days before.

"It's filthy," he said.

"Well, of course it is, Neil, if you haven't done anything about it," Tessa said, already halfway up the stairs to her studio.

"But what shall I do?" he asked.

"Put it to soak now and hang it out this afternoon when you come in. You'll remember next time. Clothes don't wash themselves."

Doing washing in a sink and hanging it out of doors was just primitive. At the Rest Home, Mum had always thrown his things in one of the big washing machines that whirred all day in the laundry room. Now he wouldn't have any clean kit for PE today, and that would mean more trouble. It seemed like the last straw.

But perhaps it wasn't any of those things that made him decide. Perhaps he'd known from the moment he'd told Wayne Penna those names that he wasn't going to go to school the next day.

Whatever the reason, he went down Ship Street as usual to catch the bus. Then he found himself going the other way. He ran up a steep flight of steps, went into the maze of narrow streets that took him around the back of the village and eventually came out on the South West Coast Path and the cliffs.

Now he looked up at the next stretch of the path. It went steeply up over the headland, winding between rocks to the high point of the cliffs. There was some sort of small shelter at the top.

He plodded up, stopping several times to get his breath back. As he came near the top he could see the next stretch, going steeply down again, then on round the edge of the next headland, keeping close to the sea. Halfway along this stretch there was a purple and white speck amid all the green undergrowth. After a moment he realised it was the woman who'd spoken to him. She must be sitting on a rock. He looked for the dog, but perhaps it was snuffling round in the bushes, or perhaps it was just too small to see.

He came up level with the shelter. Now he was closer he could see that it was made of grey concrete and its foundations were set deep inside the hillside. Its stained walls looked blank and solid. But when he walked round to the side away from the sea he discovered two or three crumbling steps leading down to a low entrance.

Peering in, he saw in the middle of the far wall a narrow slit like a letter box. He suddenly realised what the building was. It was an old look-out post, the sort of thing that was built in the Second World War so people could watch the sea for signs that the Nazis might be coming to invade.

He ducked inside. The sudden chill and the dank smell hit him. It seemed almost completely dark to him, coming in as he was from the bright sunshine of the cliffs. He went over to the viewing slit, stood on tiptoe and looked out.

He saw a wide stretch of sea, right to the horizon. He watched a small fishing boat that had come round the headland from Portmartin dipping and rising in the water, leaving a foaming white wake behind it. It stopped at a yellow marker buoy. The man on board was moving about but it was too far away for Neil to see what he was doing.

It felt odd, looking out at him like that. The man on that boat didn't know he was being watched. If he should happen to look across at the land from out there, he'd never notice a pair of eyes staring at him through the slit. It was like being a spy, Neil thought, rather pleased with the idea.

He turned to go. Just as he reached the door, a voice behind him said,

"Hello, Neil."

3

He gasped and whipped round.

"Annis?"

She was hunched in the corner, arms around her knees, her school bag beside her.

He went nearer. "You freaked me out," he said. "What are you doing here?"

"What are *you*?" She looked up at him. "This is my place, not yours."

He didn't know what to say. He backed towards the entrance. "OK, I'm going. I don't like it here much anyway."

"I do." She looked round at the bare grey walls. "It's safe in here."

He stared at her. "How do you mean, safe?"

She put her head down. "Just safe."

He waited. She didn't say anything else. After a minute he said, "I'm going now."

"Where?"

He shrugged. "Just on, I suppose."

He went out, turned his back on Portmartin and started walking down the rough path. The sun had gone in and the wind was chilly. He pushed his hands in his pockets and turned up his collar.

In a minute or two he heard feet running behind him. He turned round.

"I'll come with you," Annis said. "If you don't mind."

"OK," he said.

They walked on together. He looked back over his shoulder. The empty path behind them stretched back up the hill, and the look-out point stood out sharply against the sky.

"Have you done it before?" Annis said after a while.

"Done what?"

She looked at him sideways. "Bunking off school."

"No," he said. "No, of course I haven't. It's just that –"

"What?"

"It's only for today," he said, though he didn't know if it was or not. "There was a reason I didn't want to go today."

"What reason?"

He shook his head. "I can't tell you."

She'd find out soon. Half the school would know soon that he had given those names to Wayne Penna.

I have done it before, he thought. *I did it in London the day I came down here. That was bunking off school.*

He went on trudging down the path to the bottom with Annis, feeling depressed. There was a stile to climb and a muddy little wooden bridge over a stream and then the path went on steeply up again to skirt round the side of the next headland.

He thought back to that day. He remembered how he'd felt about coming to The Hermit Shell when he was on the *Cornish Riviera*. He'd felt that if only he could get inside the house and hide, nothing else would ever go wrong.

But it had gone wrong. Exactly the same things had gone wrong again. Trouble at school, trouble at home. He'd run away to leave his problems behind, but somehow he'd brought them with him

4

The cliffs were very steep on this stretch of path, dropping sheer a long way down to the sea. The path round the headland was narrow and in places they had to pick their way round rocks and boulders. Sea birds circled the cliff sides, screaming and calling.

"Annis?"

"Yes?"

"The days you don't go to school . . . " Neil spoke very carefully, hoping she wouldn't fly at him. "Why? I mean . . . why some days and not others?"

She stood still, frowning, not answering.

"It could be something wrong at school," he went on. "But you've got lots of friends and you can do all the work, so I don't think it's that. You're not afraid of anything at school, are you?" She couldn't be afraid as he was afraid.

"School's all right," she said.

"So there's some other reason," he said. "I think it's something to do with the lifeboat. It is, isn't it?"

She gave a quick, unwilling nod.

"I thought so. I've just worked it out. The day you stay away is always the day after your dad's been out on a shout."

"Not after every shout," she said quickly.

"No, because perhaps you can't manage that. You can't do it too often or you'll get caught. But several times lately there's been a shout, and you haven't gone to school the next day. That's true, isn't it?"

They faced each other on the cliff path. Her hair blew over her face.

"Yes," she said.

"Why?" said Neil. "I don't understand."

There was a long silence. Over her shoulder, Neil saw a rabbit scampering away into the bramble bushes. Out at sea, the fishing boat had stopped at another yellow buoy.

"Promise you won't tell anyone," said Annis.

"OK."

She said in a small voice, "I have to make sure Dad's all right." She lifted her eyes and looked straight at him. "That's what I'm doing, OK?"

"But ..." he said. "How can you make sure he's all right?"

Annis was walking on down the path. Over her shoulder she said, "It's a very dangerous job, you know, on the lifeboat. You get gales along this coast, you haven't seen them yet. Awful storms come up suddenly from nowhere, and the lifeboat has to go out in them. Other people go indoors and shut their windows and pull the bedclothes over their heads, but my dad and the rest go out into all that sea to rescue people. It can be really dangerous."

He hurried after her.

"I know. But I still don't see –"

"Well," she said, "there's a shout. And that starts me thinking. I think about how they might go out one day and ... not come back."

"They always do," Neil argued. "I mean, I know about the lifeboat that was lost, but that was years and years ago."

"It could happen again," she said. "It might. Sometimes when Dad goes out I wonder if it will, and I think I won't go to school next day, because suppose it happened then and I wasn't here? So I pretend to catch the bus and then I come and spend the day up here."

"The whole day?" said Neil wonderingly.

She shrugged.

"It's the best place, out of people's way. If anyone saw me in the village they might tell Dad. I walk around or I just sit down somewhere and read. I spend quite a lot of time in there." She pointed up at the look-out post. "Sometimes I stand for ages looking out, watching the sea. Like you did this morning. Some days I see the lifeboat going out. Then I watch till it comes back safely. It's always good when I can do that. Then I know, you see."

Neil's eyes widened.

"Don't you get cold?"

"Well, of course I do," she said. "It's freezing sometimes. I eat my school sandwiches and I keep looking at my watch and . . . Once I was so tired looking out that I lay down and had a sleep. Only once. I keep myself awake now till it's time to go down and pretend I've just got off the bus."

"And your dad thinks you've been at school all day," said Neil.

"That's the easy bit," she said. "Dad asks if I've had a good day and I just say yes. Mum was different. She always asked a lot about school. But Dad doesn't. Dad's too busy with the lifeboat."

"And the absence notes?" asked Neil.

"I do them on the computer up in my room."

"And sign your dad's signature?"

"Well, I have to," she said. "I practised a lot and now I'm really good at it."

"But that's forgery," said Neil.

"Don't call it that," said Annis. She began to walk on very fast, leaving him behind.

He couldn't get used to the idea that Annis was leading this secret life that nobody else knew about. It sounded awful. He ran to catch her up.

"Look, why don't you tell your dad how you feel?" he asked. "He ought to know how scared you are, and how you keep missing school. Or tell Tessa. You could tell Tessa, couldn't you?"

"I'm not telling anyone," she said. "There'd be all sorts of trouble."

"There wouldn't." Neil was still running to keep up. He had to help Annis stop doing such awful things, truanting and forging letters and deceiving Mat. "I'll tell them for you if you like."

"You mustn't," she cried. "You promised. Go away. This is my place, not yours. I never asked you to interfere." She broke into a run. "I wish I'd never told you now. You promised you wouldn't tell anyone."

"I didn't know what you were going to say then," Neil argued. "I'm only trying to help."

She spun round.

"You aren't . . . You mustn't –" and then, with one frightened gasp she was gone, rolling and sliding over the edge of the path and the edge of the cliff and he heard her screaming and screaming.

He stood alone in the middle of the path, too terrified even to move.

CHAPTER SEVEN

Waiting

Perhaps he stood there a long time, his hands pressed to his mouth, perhaps only a few seconds. But at last he made himself move to the side of the path and look over the edge of the cliff.

The cliff fell steeply to the sea, a dizzying drop of bare rock face and ledges where a few small bushes and plants clung.

There was no sign of Annis.

"Annis?" he called, his hands cupped round his mouth. "Where are you? Annis!"

He listened, and heard nothing but the crying of seagulls. He turned his head frantically, looking along the path for someone to help him. He ran a few steps, first one way and then the other, gasping for breath. She must be dead. This couldn't be happening. It couldn't.

"ANNIS!"

Was there a faint answer this time, coming from a long way down? He strained his ears.

"Help me . . . Help . . . Neil . . ."

He dropped to a sitting position with his legs over the edge of the cliff and began to slither down on his back, digging in with his heels, his hands grabbing at gorse bushes or jutting rocks or a handful of grass – anything to slow himself down, to save him from tumbling helplessly all the way to the bottom like Annis. Loose pebbles rolled under him and his spine bumped painfully over the hard ground. His sleeve caught on a thorn bush. He tore it free and went on slithering down.

"Neil, I'm here. Oh, it hurts . . . Neil, help me."

He could see her now, a crumpled dark-blue shape. She was still a long way below him, right down near the water.

"Hang on. I'm coming."

He slithered and rolled, snatched at a plant and felt it give way and went on sliding until a sharp rock stopped him going any further.

"*Ow*."

He clutched his knee where he'd banged it on the rock. Then he sat up and looked across at Annis.

She was lying almost in the water, on her back between two rocks. Her head was tilted towards the sea and her legs were twisted under her.

"Neil . . . thank goodness."

He edged nearer. Now he was actually down there with her he didn't feel quite so bad.

"Are you all right?"

"My leg," she said, struggling to lift herself. "It's jammed somehow. I can't get up."

"I'll help you." He took hold of her clumsily and tried to haul her up.

"Don't, don't," she screamed. "You're hurting me, Neil. Let go."

"Sorry."

"I'm stuck . . . my leg . . . this rock . . . Get it off me please, Neil . . . please . . ."

He could see her left leg looked all wrong. It was bent at a funny angle and wedged between the rocks. He put his shoulder against one rock and heaved. Nothing happened. He tried again.

"Can't you move it?"

She started crying. Tears trickled down her face, mixing with blood from where she'd scraped her cheek. Her eyes looked huge and she was very pale. "I can't bear to be stuck. I must move. Please, Neil –"

"All right. It'll be all right."

He stood up and scanned the cliffs. Nothing moved. He remembered with a sinking feeling that the woman with the dog had said they had the cliffs to themselves that morning.

He turned round. The cliffs rose straight out of the sea in each direction. There was no escape that way. He looked out to sea.

"That fishing boat's still there," he said.

"That's Dave Ollis, doing his lobster pots. I was watching him earlier. He'll help us. Shout to him."

Neil climbed on a rock and waved. He shouted till his throat was sore. The boat moved steadily away.

After a time Annis said, "He hasn't heard you, has he?"

"No. Never mind."

As he climbed off the rock, he noticed how terribly close Annis's head was to the sea. The breaking waves were almost splashing her hair. He tried to remember the state of the tide. If it was rising, before long the water would come right up over her face. He wouldn't be able to move her and she would drown. He made a decision.

"I'm going to get help."

She clutched at him. "Don't leave me."

"Annis, I've got to. I won't be long."

But when he tried to climb back the way he'd come he couldn't get a foothold. Again and again he slipped back. He swore under his breath.

Annis twisted her head. "Haven't you gone yet? What's the matter?"

"I can't do it. It's too slippery." Neil sat down beside her. "Too steep."

"So what are we going to do?"

He didn't have an answer. They looked at each other in

silence. Then Annis said,

"Listen."

A dog was barking somewhere high on the cliff. He heard someone whistle to it.

"Who is it?"

"I don't know." Neil was on his feet. He couldn't see anyone up there. "Shout. Shout with me."

"HELP!" Together they shouted at the tops of their voices. Then again. And again.

They waited.

Neil's heart was thudding. If there was no answer they were stuck. He was sure now the tide was coming in. If nobody else came they would both drown. Annis first, then him.

"Hello?"

To his huge relief, a purple-and-white shape had appeared at the edge of the cliff above him. It was the woman he had seen before. She must have been on her way back to Portmartin. He waved frantically.

"We're . . . STUCK." He pointed at Annis and mimed her injured leg. "Can you . . . get . . . HELP?"

She waved back and gestured that she was coming down.

"No!" He tried to shoo her back up with his hands. Even if she made it to the bottom, she'd never climb up again. Then they'd all be stuck down there.

After one or two uncertain movements she seemed, to his relief, to give up. She began shouting and gesturing with her stick.

" . . . Try . . . be quick . . . " Her words floated away.

"Don't worry . . . Stay there . . ."

She disappeared. The dog barked once, then again further away. Then he didn't hear it again.

Stay there, thought Neil. What else could he and Annis do? He looked at his watch. He wondered how far away the nearest telephone was.

Whatever happened, it looked as if they were in for a long wait.

3

Annis's teeth were chattering. Neil took off his jacket and covered her with it.

"How's your leg?" he asked.

"Sort of stiff and funny. My face hurts the worst. And my elbow. I really banged it when I fell."

He looked at his watch again. They'd only been waiting seven minutes. "Someone will come soon," he said.

"The lifeboat probably," said Annis. "Dad and the lifeboat. So he'll find out I'm not at school." She gave a twisted smile. "That argument we had up there was a waste of time, because Dad's going to find out everything now. Everything about what I've been doing."

And about me, thought Neil. Tessa, and the school and everyone. They're all going to know.

He would have run away then if he could. But he couldn't get up the cliff, and there was nowhere else to run and, anyway, how could he leave Annis on her own?

There was no doubt now that the tide was coming in.

Water was creeping round the rocks behind Annis's head, nearly touching the end of her hair where it hung down. She didn't seem to notice. Perhaps being in pain took up all her attention.

"Hey, don't go to sleep." Her eyelids were drooping. He felt urgently that she must keep awake.

She opened her eyes and frowned.

"Where are you?"

"Here." He'd moved round, kneeling behind her head to keep the spray off her. He looked at his watch again. Twelve minutes. He must keep her talking.

"They'll be in the middle of French at school."

No answer.

"French, then lunch. Are you hungry?"

"I feel sick."

He glanced over his shoulder at the empty sea. The spray was splashing him now. The back of his shirt was wet. He was freezing.

"The lifeboat will soon be here." He tried to stop his teeth chattering. "Tell me about the lifeboat."

"Leave me alone."

"Come on, Annis. Tell me how fast it can go."

She groaned. "Neil, don't . . ."

"How fast, Annis? How fast does it go?"

Her eyes dragged open. "I don't remember . . . 16, 17 knots? Pretty fast . . ."

He was afraid she'd drift off again, but once he got her talking he found he could keep her going. In a strange, half-mumbling voice she began telling him about the engines, about how the boat would turn itself the right way up if it capsized, about the radar and computers on board, about some of the shouts she remembered.

"When I was little, I used to love seeing the boat go roaring out. Sometimes Mum and I would stand on the harbour wall and watch, and I used to laugh and clap and jump up and down. Then we'd wait at home, and I always knew he'd come back. I was such a stupid little kid." Her laugh turned into a sob. "I used to really love it."

"But now you hate it, don't you?" Neil said. "When the boat goes out, you're scared. You're even scared to take *Gannet* out."

The sea was swirling all round him now. He was kneeling in water. He had to lean close to hear her reply.

"It's different now. I don't like the sea any more. Since Mum died last year . . . Since she was in hospital –" She twisted her head. "My hair's sopping wet. What is it?"

"Nothing," said Neil. "It's all right. Go on. Since your mum was in hospital . . .?"

Slowly at first, then more easily, Annis began to talk. Her mother had been in hospital for two or three weeks, very ill. Annis and Mat had gone to visit her every evening. Then one evening she'd seemed different. Not more ill, exactly. Just different.

"I didn't say anything," Annis whispered, "but I thought about it all night. I knew something was going to happen to her. Next morning, the hospital called to say she was worse and Dad went rushing over there. I wanted to go with him but everyone said I should go to school. They kept saying that's what Mum would . . . would want me to do . . . "

She was sobbing now, her hands twisting. "So I went to school and she died. She died that morning."

"That's awful," said Neil. Behind him, there was the throb of a boat's engines now, and the sound was getting closer.

"Yes, it was." The tears spilled down her face. "I wanted to be with my mum, and I wasn't. And that's why I don't go to school sometimes now. Ever since then, I've been so worried about Dad, because of what happened to Mum. Dad's all I've got now. Suppose something went wrong on a shout? Suppose he didn't come back? If something happened, I couldn't bear to be in school. It would be just like my mum all over again."

"But you've just been telling me how safe the lifeboat is," Neil protested. "Nothing'll happen to your dad."

"It might. You never know. I'm not risking it."

"But . . ."

Neil suddenly knew what all this reminded him of. It was the same as him trying to creep into a shell like a hermit crab and block the entrance. He and Annis were the same. They were both trying to make life absolutely safe for themselves. Trying to make sure nothing would ever hurt them again.

"Why don't you tell your dad all this?" he asked.

"He wouldn't listen," said Annis. "He's too busy."

The roar of engines was tremendous now. Neil looked over his shoulder to see *Dolly Hescomb* turning, a curtain of white spray flying up from her navy-blue hull. Even as she came to rest a little way off the cliffs, the crew were lowering a small inflatable craft over the side.

"Are they here?" Annis whispered.

"Yes. Someone's coming." He stood up stiffly, raising his arms to signal to the inflatable. It moved towards him. Under the helmsman's white helmet he recognised Wayne Penna. Radio messages crackled backwards and forwards across the water:

"Portmartin Lifeboat to Falmouth Coastguard . . ."
"Go ahead Portmartin . . ."
"We have located the two casualties at base of cliffs. We are landing a first aider from the crew to investigate. Over."
"All received and understood, Portmartin."

Neil watched the inflatable come into land. Wayne Penna secured the craft, and came across the rocks towards them, carrying a first aid kit. He spoke into a radio round his neck.

"OK, Mat. I'm with the casualties now, two children, one male, one female. I am about to . . . about to . . . "

Then he stopped in mid-message, looking down at Annis, looking up at Neil, looking down at Annis again. He shook his head in disbelief. Then he spoke into his microphone again.

" . . . about to assess the situation," he said. *"There's just one thing first. The female casualty, Mat. I'm afraid it's Annis. Repeat, the female casualty is your daughter, Annis."*

After that, everything happened very fast. To Neil, it all seemed to be taking place in a blur, almost as if he were watching it happen to someone else.

The thing that mattered more than anything, said Wayne, was to keep Annis's face above the incoming water until her leg could be freed. So Neil supported her head and shoulders in the way Wayne showed him, and Wayne gently examined her damaged leg and made urgent radio calls explaining the situation. Then, while Wayne went back to the lifeboat, Neil stayed with Annis. He tried to shelter her from the splashing waves, and to keep talking as calmly as he could.

Then Wayne came back with Mat, and Annis was crying on her father's shoulder and Mat was saying that everything was all right now, that the helicopter would be there any minute, that soon Annis would be safe in hospital.

It seemed that the next moment there was a throbbing in the air. Neil looked round. A helicopter was skimming low over the sea, turning in towards them. As it came closer they were deafened by sound, caught up in the huge downdraught of air that nearly blew them away. It edged nearer and nearer, hovering, then the door opened and a man was being winched down.

He landed close by, and the three men worked rapidly, giving Annis an injection, testing her reflexes for injury, fitting a collar to protect her neck. Wayne and Mat together forced the rocks apart to free her leg.

"Easy, now, easy."

"You're doing well. Good girl. Soon be done."

Hearing her cry out with pain, Neil knew how much it hurt her. But at last she was free. Soon she was strapped into a stretcher and the stretcher was fastened to the winch.

The winch man looked at Mat. "Are you coming with her, or going back with the boat, Mat?"

Just briefly, Mat's eyes flicked out to the lifeboat. Then he met Annis's pleading eyes and touched her hand.

"No question about that," he said. "Wayne and the lads can take the boat back. They'll cope just this once."

Before Neil took in what was happening, Annis had gone, rising above their heads. The winch man was with her, his body protecting her from bumps. The two of them gently turned in the air, rising, rising, until they reached the helicopter's open door and waiting hands gathered them in. Then the winch came down again for Mat and he too was gone.

With a roar, the helicopter turned and the door closed. Already it was moving out of sight, rising above the cliffs. The throb of its engines faded . . . died.

"Right, Neil," said Wayne. "Back home quick."

Neil stumbled over the rocks towards the inflatable. He was soaked to the skin, shaking with cold and, now it was nearly over, shock. He would have fallen if Wayne's arm hadn't steadied him.

On board *Dolly Hescomb* there were warm blankets, a drink that scalded his throat, men's voices all round.

"Portmartin Lifeboat to Falmouth Coastguard . . ."
"Go ahead, Portmartin . . ."
"Service completed. Will be returning to station shortly."
"All received and understood, Portmartin."

He sat with Wayne, hugging the blankets round him, feeling the boat powering back round the coast to Portmartin.

"Really caught me out this morning, that shout did," Wayne said. "I was just going over to The Sailor's Return for a pint with one of my mates when my pager went off."

"Sorry," said Neil.

Wayne shrugged. "I'll have the pint tonight with luck. Anyway, it all worked out all right, though it costs a packet to have the helicopter out. But you know what?"

"What?"

"Annis would have died without you. No question of that. You did everything right."

"Did I?"

"You didn't run off. You went down to the bottom and stayed with her. You made contact with someone who could call us out. You helped me when I came. No hysteria, no ab-dabs, nothing like that." He smiled. "We'll make a crewman of you one day."

They were slowing down now, coming in to harbour. Neil was surprised to see it was still light, only lunch time, really. It seemed so long since breakfast, since deciding to miss the bus. Almost like a different day.

"Course, you shouldn't have been up on the cliffs

116

this morning," Wayne remarked. "Bunking off school, were you?"

Neil nodded. A small hope came to him. Perhaps Wayne hadn't really meant it when he'd said he'd tell the school about the damage they'd done yesterday.

"Wayne, that phone call you said you'd do. You know, to the school –"

"Did it first thing today," said Wayne. "If I say a thing, I mean it. Sorry."

"Oh."

Wayne looked down at him. "Don't worry now," he said. "I reckon you'll go to school tomorrow, and you'll be all right." He stood up. "Look, we're in. And there's someone coming to meet you."

Neil looked out. Tessa was racing down the hill, hair flying. A moment later he was out of the boat and enveloped in a big hug.

5

For the rest of the day he didn't want to be left on his own.

Tessa made him lie down on the sofa, tucked under a duvet with a hot water bottle. She even tried to get him to drink hot milk.

"Are you sure you're not hurt, Neil?" she kept saying. "Why don't you go to bed for a while?"

But he couldn't have slept. His mind still whirred with the morning's events: being suddenly alone at the top of the cliffs when Annis vanished; the sound of her scream when he tried to move her; the feel of the sea swirling round him, creeping higher and higher, threatening to drown them both.

Tessa sat with him. After a time he could feel her fidgeting. "Look, Neil," she said at last, "I do have to go down to the gallery in a minute. I'm doing an interview for a London magazine and they'll be waiting for me. I'll be as quick as I can. Perhaps you could sleep while I'm gone."

"I could come with you," he said.

"Oh, no, Neil. That wouldn't –"

"Please," he said.

"You must wrap up well, then."

They walked down Ship Street together. He felt quite shy of her; he'd never seen her in a dress before and her hair was done in a completely different way.

There were signs pointing along the street where the art gallery was: TESSA LOFTUS. ONE-WOMAN SHOW – *SEA-JUNGLE*.

The gallery, with its light, high-ceilinged rooms, was full of people.

"I couldn't believe how well the opening went this morning," Tessa said, smiling at people as she led the way through. "Crowds of visitors, three pictures sold in the first hour, wonderful speeches – "

"About *you*?"

"Why not?" said Tessa, grinning at him.

She took a glass of wine from a table and poured a drink for Neil. "Why don't you sit and wait for me a minute?"

Instead, he wandered round, looking at her pictures. In some of them, he could recognise Portmartin: the top of the church tower, a gull and a scrap of fishing net, the harbour rails. Looking at the rails, he gradually recognised the red and white outline of *Gannet* down in the harbour. Then he saw himself at the oars, Annis in the stern. He'd had no idea Tessa had ever watched them.

He looked up. Across the gallery she was being photographed, wine glass in hand, laughing. Then she came over to him.

"What do you think of the pictures, Neil? Are they OK?" She sounded quite anxious to know.

"Once you're used to them," he said. "Then you see things." He pointed at the splodgy blue and green picture she'd been so anxious about on hanging day.

"That's Dead Men's Ropes in that one," he said.

"Right. Dead Men's Ropes that I had in my bucket on the day you came."

"And . . . a horse? Oh, and the antlers. And a sort of spear thing."

"It's a hunt. An undersea hunt."

He was baffled. "Why?"

"Oh, because . . . It's a jungle under the sea, everything eating everything, no hiding place."

"Unless you're a hermit crab," said Neil, "in a shell."

"Maybe." Tessa looked uncertain. "Or maybe you're safer if you come out and face things. Then you don't need to hide." She laughed. "Though *I* can't talk. I've got to do a really frightening thing in a minute. I've got to ring your mother and tell her what happened this morning."

"Don't –"

"Your parents have to be told," said Tessa. "But I really

119

dread it, Neil. Can't you just see the headlines in your dad's head? *Weirdo Artist Lets Boy Fall From Cliff* . . . Neil, I dread it." She finished her wine gloomily.

"You didn't let me fall," said Neil. "I didn't fall at all. I'm OK. I'm going to school tomorrow."

"Sure?" She raised an eyebrow. "You've got trouble there, haven't you? Like you had in London?"

"A bit."

"Perhaps you should run away again," she said, looking at him.

"Nowhere to run to," said Neil. "I'm at the end of England."

She squeezed his arm.

"I'll make that phone call tonight," she said, "and tell you how I get on. You go to school tomorrow, and tell me how you get on. OK?"

Before they went home, they called in at the hospital to ask about Annis.

"A nasty fracture, and cuts and bruises," they said at the desk. "No head injuries as far as we can tell. But we're keeping her in tonight."

They found Annis, leg in plaster, propped up in bed with her dad's arm round her. The two of them were so busy talking that they didn't even notice Tessa and Neil walking down the ward towards them.

CHAPTER EIGHT

Dead Calm

Before long it was spring. The hedges were thick with primroses, and daffodils stood in buckets outside the flower shops of Penzance. Then Easter came and, with Easter, the 'Bed and Breakfast' signs went up in Portmartin and the first visitors arrived. Then suddenly it was summer, and the holiday season was in full swing.

"Them emmets," grumbled some of the old people. "Foreigners swarming all over Cornwall. The English ought to keep t'other side of the River Tamar, give us a bit o' quiet."

That wasn't the way Wayne Penna saw things. For him, summer was the best time of the year.

One July afternoon, Neil came hurrying into Penna's

Café. Every table was full, and people were jostling round the ice-cream freezer and the counter.

'Hi, Neil," called Wayne. "Bit busy here. Be with you in a minute."

"OK."

Neil stood where he could look out of the window at the harbour and the bus stop, and waited till Wayne was free to talk.

"This is the way I like it." Wayne looked round with satisfaction, wiping the counter as he spoke. "Got to make a bob or two while summer lasts. I've got my mum and dad out the back today, doing the washing up."

The Pennas were a large family. There was always someone to help out when things got busy in the summer, or to stand in when Wayne was called out to the lifeboat.

"Right then, Neil, what's for you? Cream tea? Lobster salad?"

"Just an ice-cream while I'm waiting."

"Help yourself," said Wayne. "Heard your school term ended yesterday."

"Yes," said Neil, rummaging in the freezer. "We're going out in *Gannet* this afternoon to celebrate."

He perched on a stool in the corner, licking his ice-cream, watching the crowds of holiday-makers trailing past the window with their beach mats and lilos and surf boards. It was hard to believe the long summer holidays were here already. Time had gone so fast since Annis's accident on the cliffs. Fast, that is, once the first few days back at school after the accident had been lived through. Those days had gone very slowly indeed. Neil didn't think he would ever forget them.

He'd been very nervous, walking into school that morning, not knowing if anything had happened to the other three yet. As luck would have it, the first people he'd bumped into in the cloakroom had been Danny and Pete and Craig.

"Hi ya, Lofty." They were as friendly as ever. "You sick yesterday, or something?"

"Something like that."

He tried to laugh and joke with them as usual but it was a strain. He could hardly believe they didn't notice. The whole morning he waited for something to happen. When by lunch time nothing had, he began to relax. Perhaps nothing would happen. But then, with startling suddenness, it did.

One minute he was leaving class with everyone else. The next minute he'd been whisked into the year head's office with the other three and was being confronted by Wayne's phone message. Confronted and accused.

"Damaging lifeboat equipment." The year head behind his desk stared down at the names on his paper, then up at them. "I've waited until today to speak to you because I wanted to check the facts and see you all together. I simply cannot understand how boys from this school could even think of running riot like that, damaging life-saving equipment. You're all Cornish boys – well, except for Neil who perhaps doesn't understand these things. But –"

"Wasn't us, sir." Danny was red-faced, his fists clenched. "I don't live nowhere near Portmartin. Nor does Pete. Who said it was us?"

He darted a furious glance at Neil. Neil quailed.

"Nothing to do with me," said Pete.

"Craig?"

Craig looked at his feet, saying nothing.

"Neil?"

Neil's heart was thudding. Slowly, he nodded.

He went on standing there while the year head spoke of the shame to the school and to all of them, of apologies and making amends. But he didn't hear one word because all he was aware of was Danny's scorn and anger scorching the back of his neck.

At last they were sent out.

"*Grasser*," hissed Danny in the empty corridor. "You told on us, you rotten, stinking grass." His foot came out and struck Neil's leg, sending him staggering into the wall. "We're going to tell everybody what you did, squealing and grassing. Your life isn't going to be worth living in this school now."

"Get back to London, squealer." Pete tried to kick him too. But at that moment the office door behind him opened and they all made off.

And, really, that had been the end of Neil being one of the gang.

He finished his ice-cream and looked out of the café window. Annis was just crossing the street. The plaster had been off her leg for some time now and he noticed she was no longer walking with a limp. He went to the door.

"I'm in here," he called. "I thought we could buy some food to take with us."

"Have you got any money?"

"A bit." He dug in his pockets. Between them, they found enough to buy crisps, drinks and three saffron buns.

"Here's the bus," said Annis, as they picked up their shopping.

Neil looked up. The bus had already put down its passengers by the harbour and was turning round to go back. The café door opened.

"Hello, Lofty."

"Hi, Craig," said Neil. "You all right?"

"Yep." Craig never wasted words. "I'm OK, mate. I'm fine."

2

Even now, Neil was hardly used to the idea that he and Craig were friends, proper friends. There'd been a time when it had seemed nobody but Annis wanted to be Neil's friend.

Word had spread quickly at school about what Neil had done – Danny and Pete saw to that.

"Heard what that Loftus did to us?"

"He's a grasser."

"Traitor."

"Tell-tale."

"Teachers' pet."

Suddenly, Neil's pens and shoes and books started to go missing. Sometimes in class, nobody wanted to sit next to him or be in a group with him. Often at break he found himself alone. When Annis came back to school, if she talked to him she got called names too. It made him feel bad, nearly as bad as he'd felt in his London school. But there didn't seem to be anything he could do about it.

It worried Tessa too when he told her about it. "That's tough, Neil. Why not let me talk to your teachers?"

Neil shook his head. That would be seen as grassing too, and only make things worse. He'd just have to ride it out, like riding out a storm.

Then, after several weeks, something happened.

They'd been doing a project at school about aspects of safety. One of the tasks had been to research safety in a particular context – safety in the home, for instance, or aircraft safety – and then to do a presentation on it to everyone. They could work in pairs or small groups. The teacher left them to arrange that for themselves.

Neil had nobody to work with. Annis wasn't in the same class for this. He'd asked one or two people but nobody had responded and then it was too late. When the day came for his presentation, he sat waiting his turn with a sinking heart, listening to Danny and Pete and Craig talking about car safety.

Then it was his turn.

"Who did you work with, Neil?" asked the teacher.

"Nobody." He gathered his stuff and went to the front. "Just me."

He saw Danny nudge Pete, grinning.

"Off you go then."

"It's about safety at sea," he said.

He fixed some pictures to the wall behind him and began. While he was talking he turned to point to one of the pictures and it fell down. There was a stifled laugh. When he tried to hold up a chart it was too big to hold on his own and he dropped it. Stooping to pick it up, he floundered over what he was saying.

The teacher got up. "Need some help, Neil?"

"No, I'm all right –"

"I'll help him."

It was Craig, stolid, silent Craig, heaving himself out of his seat next to Danny, coming to the front to stand with Neil. He helped hold the chart so everyone could see. He fastened the pictures more firmly to the wall and pointed things out as Neil mentioned them. And when, at the end of the lesson, Danny called him away, Craig ignored him and went on helping Neil clear up.

"Come *on*, Craig. He's a grasser, remember?"

Craig looked up. "No, I don't remember none o' that." He rolled up the chart and handed it to Neil.

When the others had gone he said to Neil, "How d'you find out all that stuff about the sea?"

"Oh, talking to Mat Boswell and the lifeboat crew," said Neil. "They've told me lots of things lately."

"Right," said Craig. He'd looked at Neil thoughtfully. "Good stuff, that. I wouldn't mind learning stuff like that."

Now, inside Penna's Café, Annis and Craig and Wayne were talking to Neil about Portmartin's summer carnival.

"Never heard of Portmartin carnival?" marvelled Wayne. "Famous throughout Cornwall, isn't it, Annis? Folk come from miles around."

127

"But what is it?"

"It's a regatta. We all get out in boats."

"And there's fund raising for the lifeboat. Everybody dresses up."

"There's a band. A procession. And prizes."

"And this year, mate," said Wayne, "You're taking part."

"Me?" said Neil.

"You."

Wayne had a plan, it seemed. He and Neil would dress up, would walk alongside the procession and collect money for the lifeboat.

"Dress up as what?"

"Clowns."

"Pirates."

"Cornish piskies," said Wayne. "Little old traditional Cornish piskies."

"You're not serious?" said Neil, horrified.

He laughed. "You'll see. I'll sort something out. Now – back to today. You'll want lifejackets."

In the summer, Wayne hired out boats to visitors and he kept a stock of lifejackets in his back room.

"Best be on the safe side," he said, writing down where they were going and what time they expected to be back.

"Bye then, Wayne."

"Cheers, Wayne."

"See you, piskies," said Wayne. "Enjoy yourselves."

They went out and picked their way through the crowds to reach the harbour. All round the edge the boatmen were shouting for custom.

"Mackerel fishing. Anyone for mackerel fishing?"

"Shark fishing. Leaving now."

"Come on now. A boat trip to see the seals."

"Evening cruise to Land's End and back. Get your tickets here."

Annis led the way to *Gannet*, and unchained her from the railings. They turned the boat right side up, carried her between them down the slipway and launched her into the water. They pulled on their lifejackets.

"Right," said Annis, holding onto the boat while they climbed in. "Let's go."

3

Later, Neil was to remember that first afternoon of the school holidays as a golden afternoon.

The three of them took *Gannet* just along the coast to a little cove Annis knew. It could only be reached by boat, or by walking over the cliffs and coming down a steep footpath and dozens of steps. Because of this, Annis and Neil and Craig had it to themselves.

They took it in turns to row. Neil went first, to show how much he'd improved in the time Annis had let him use *Gannet* on his own while she'd been out of action, then Craig, to give him some practice. Craig had been coming over to Portmartin whenever he could in the last few weeks, and Annis said he had the makings of a good rower, strong and steady. But he still needed to remember to look over his shoulder more often at where he was going, she said, or he'd be in trouble.

Coming out of the harbour, Annis had taken over, to prove to everyone that her leg really was strong enough now, and to negotiate the tricky currents. Then the boys took an oar each, pulling steadily, while Annis set a course close to the shore. Waves had been whipped up by the westerly wind into peaks like meringue.

"Hey, this is great," said Neil, looking at the empty sand and the clear blue water as they came in close to shore.

"Yeah, it's all right that," said Craig. "Hang on. I just got to cool off."

He shipped his oar, stripped off his lifejacket and shirt, and climbed onto the stern seat, poised ready to dive.

"Come on," he shouted. "Last one in's a babby."

"Go on, then," said Neil and with a push toppled him in.

Craig was one of the best swimmers in the school. He came up spluttering and shouting and made a grab for Neil. Soon all three of them were in the water around the boat, swimming and splashing. Then they hauled themselves over the side and lay rocking in the sun for a while before tumbling in again.

Later, they dragged *Gannet* up the beach and lolled on the rocks, eating and drinking and talking about what they were going to do in the holidays.

"Maybe – just maybe –" said Annis, "Dad and I will go to my auntie's on Exmoor for a week. It's really great there. They live on a farm and there are all these ponies to ride and you can see deer on the moor. I usually go on my own. But this time I really think Dad might take a break and come with me."

Craig told them about the holiday camp he was going to

with his family. It had a fantastic swimming pool and three giant water slides and everything.

Neil himself was going up to London to see his parents for a week. He was catching a train in the morning. But he'd be back in time for the carnival.

"Lucky thing," said Craig. "I haven't never been to London."

"It'll be nice for you to go home for a while," said Annis.

Neil lay on his stomach, idly trying to prise a limpet off the rock, and thought about it. Was London home? Of course, he'd like to see his mum, and his dad, too. But he'd been in Cornwall six months now, half a year. More and more, 'home' was coming to mean not the Quiet Corner Rest Home in London, but The Hermit Shell in Portmartin. It was as if – he struggled to get this straight in his mind – as if he'd really settled down in Cornwall and was happy. Yes, that was it. After all the trouble at the beginning, he really was happy.

It wasn't that every single thing had come right that day Craig had turned his back on Danny and Pete, and started to be Neil's friend instead. It wasn't quite as simple as that. But that day had been the turning point. For a while, Danny and Pete tried to get Craig back with them. They started calling him the same sort of names they called Neil. When that didn't work, they lost interest and took up with other people. After that everyone else began to treat Neil and Craig quite normally. Perhaps most of them never had been that bothered in the first place – just afraid not to agree with Danny. Like sheep, Craig said, dozy old sheep.

Soon Neil and Craig had been too busy to think about

the past anyway. There was swimming and cricket and athletics, there were school outings to a Cornish tin mine and to Land's End, Neil had a part in the school play and Tessa came to watch him. Above all, there was Mat Boswell, Wayne Penna and the Portmartin lifeboat.

Neil spent a lot of time at the boat house now, helping out and learning, sometimes with Craig, sometimes alone. He'd learnt to recognise different sorts of shipping, and he'd learnt the names of lifeboat classes like Trent and Severn and Mersey. He knew why some lifeboats, like Portmartin's, were launched from a carriage, while others used slipways or were moored out on the water. He'd learnt the difference between MF radio and VHF radio, and why the Coastguard was the only one to have control of Channel Zero. He'd watched *Dolly Hescomb* on exercise come into harbour with all her windows blacked out, relying completely on navigational aids, and he'd learnt about breeches buoys and jackstays. Above all he'd discovered, by watching Mat and Wayne and the rest of the crew working and joking and laughing together, how strong they were and how much they all trusted each other.

"Time to go." Abruptly, Annis got to her feet and pulled on her life jacket. "The weather's going to pack in soon."

"Is it?" Neil looked at the sky. Without their noticing, clouds had been creeping in and now the sky was grey.

"There's no wind," he said.

"Looks all right to me," said Craig.

"I know." Annis was collecting the remains of their picnic. "But I think a storm's coming. The air can go dead calm like this sometimes, sort of warm and still, but there's a storm waiting out there in the Atlantic and it'll come rushing in before long. I think one's on its way."

They packed up and rowed home. Nothing happened. The sea was so calm it seemed as safe as a boating lake. But Neil had lived in Portmartin long enough to have learnt one more thing. He'd learnt the lifeboat people's feeling for the sea.

It wasn't fear, exactly. It was respect. A good healthy respect.

4

The storm did come, but not till long after Craig had gone home.

The first little skirmishes of wind flickered round the narrow streets of Portmartin just as dusk closed in. Behind them came stronger, fiercer winds rushing in from the west, setting boats rocking in the harbour, rattling windows in Penna's Café, howling round the rooftops and chimney pots of Ship Street. As the evening wore on and the tide swept in to the beach below The Hermit Shell, the wind caught up the sea and smashed it on the rocks, sending spray high in the air, then sucked the water back and smashed it again and again and again.

The storm was so noisy that the chimes of the village clock striking midnight were lost on the wind. And few people heard the sound of running feet past their windows as the lifeboat crew were summoned to the boat house, or saw Annis run across Ship Street to The Hermit Shell.

Within only a few minutes *Dolly Hescomb* had been launched and was away, heading through heavy seas for a 50-foot yacht that had reported engine failure seven miles west of Peneedle Point.

Only it wasn't west of Peneedle Point at all, as Mat discovered after searching for some time in that area and getting no response to his direction-finding operations. The people aboard the yacht had misread their position. It wasn't until the lifeboat had turned and made her way round to the other side of the Point and started searching again, that they were located, five miles *east* of the Point.

By now the wind was Gale Force 8 gusting Force 9, and the lifeboat was rising five metres on each wave, and then crashing into a trough five metres deep. When she finally reached the yacht the time was five minutes past two. The yacht was lying across wind and tide and was rolling violently. Its mizzen mast had split and its foresail was shredded.

There were six people on board, cold, frightened and seasick. Mat contacted them by radio and told them he would soon get them onto the lifeboat. Their yacht could break up at any moment.

He then went to the lifeboat's upper steering position where he could best see what he was doing. Wayne Penna and three other crew members went out to the foredeck ready to snatch the survivors as the lifeboat went in close to the yacht.

At two fifteen Mat made his first run in. The four crew members managed to snatch three survivors safely aboard before he had to back off. The second run in was aborted because the position was not right. On the third run in, at two twenty, the foredeck crew grabbed the other three survivors and hauled them aboard.

It was at that moment that Mat saw the yacht's mizzen mast start to fall towards the lifeboat.

5

"Are you awake, Neil?" Tessa put her head round the door.

"What's the time?"

"Half past six. You've got a train to catch, remember?"

"OK."

He sat up in bed and pulled back the curtain. The worst of the storm seemed to be over, but giant waves were still rolling in one behind the other and spray was being tossed high up on the rocks. Patches of blue sky were appearing as the clouds opened up.

He had packed his bag for his London holiday the night before and he only had to put in a few last-minute things. He went down his stairs on the way to the bathroom.

"Hello."

Annis was sitting on the floor in Tessa's studio, fully dressed.

"Oh, are you still here?" said Neil. "You were right about that storm. I wonder what time the crew came back."

"They aren't back."

"Oh." Neil stood still. "Well, some jobs take a long time, I expect."

"Yes, they do," said Annis. "And we'd have heard if anything had gone wrong. I'm not worried."

But he could tell she was, a bit. Since the day on the cliffs she had gone a long way in conquering her fear when the boat went out, but it would never quite leave her.

"We could have a quick breakfast and then go down to the boat house and see if there's any news," Tessa suggested. "There'll just be time before Neil has to go."

It was still early as they walked down Ship Street. They turned the corner by the harbour.

"Look." Tessa pointed.

The boat house doors were open and they could see *Dolly Hescomb* just being manoeuvred inside.

"All right now?"

"Yes." Annis gave a skip.

Tessa squeezed her hand. "Me too."

They went inside. The crew were hosing down the boat, checking equipment, restocking supplies.

"Hi," shouted Neil to a man on deck. "Got back all right, then."

"Sort of."

It was then Neil realised how quiet it was. There was none of the usual chatter and joking as they worked. He suddenly felt cold.

"What's happened?"

"The cox'll tell you. He's down in the fore cabin cleaning the floor. Two of the casualties were sick all the way back."

Mat came up on deck carrying a bucket.

"Mat," said Tessa, "did something go wrong?"

He looked down at the three of them.

"Wrong?" he said, "You could say I got it wrong. I couldn't reverse quick enough when the mast came crashing down. If I could've done, he might have been all right."

"Who would?"

"Young Wayne," said Mat. "Wayne Penna. He was all smashed up, Tess. He's in hospital and he's very, very bad."

CHAPTER NINE

No Change

Neil caught the train with only minutes to spare.

"Now, be sure to have a good time," Tessa urged him, handing up his bag. "Just enjoy being with your mum and dad and forget about the troubles here."

"I'll try," Neil promised, but he knew it wouldn't be easy. The news about Wayne had shocked everyone and he couldn't stop thinking about it. The latest report from the hospital had sounded very serious: Wayne was in a coma, his family were with him and nobody could say if he was going to get better or not. Mat, worried out of his mind, was blaming himself for the accident.

When the yacht's mast had started to fall, he had thrown the lifeboat into reverse at full speed to try to avoid it. But there wasn't time to get away. The mast had crashed down on the foredeck where Wayne and the others were standing, smashing into the deck and crushing Wayne.

"If I'd just been a bit quicker . . ." Mat had kept saying in the boat house. Someone had put a mug of tea in his hand but he hadn't attempted to drink it.

"I don't see how you could have been," Tessa told him. "You had to hold the boat close in while they took the casualties off. You took a risk going in there at all with the mast in that state. But if you hadn't taken that risk, all the people on the yacht would have died. Those six people have survived unhurt, thanks to you."

"And Wayne hasn't," said Mat. He smiled sadly. "I'm going in to the hospital now. I don't think there'll be anything I can do for Wayne, but at least I'll be there with him."

"Can I come with you?" Neil had asked. "I don't have to go to London today. I could ring Mum and say –"

But Tessa had been firm. Neil must go as he had promised or his parents would be disappointed.

He leaned out of the window as the train started to move. "Let me know, Tessa, won't you?" he called. "Let me know when Wayne starts to get better or –"

"I will. Bye!"

The platform was left behind. Neil sat back on his seat.

When Wayne gets better or doesn't get better, he thought. Those are the only two choices there are.

Be sure to have a good time, Tessa had told him, and he did his best to do that. His mother had arranged people to cover for her, and she and Neil went out on all sorts of excursions around London. They went to Madame Tussaud's to see the waxworks, they went shopping in the West End, they went down the Thames on a boat to visit the Tower of London.

In fact, they did all the sort of things that tourists in London do, and that was rather what Neil felt like: a tourist up from the country, just there to look around and then leave again.

He hadn't realised his mother saw it differently. But one hot afternoon, when they were sitting under the trees in St James's Park, watching the ducks paddling round on the lake, she suddenly said, "It's nice, isn't it, having these days out together? That's what I need, you know, to take more time off, not rush round all day like I used to. That was most of the trouble, the trouble between Dad and me and everything. We just never stopped working. But that's over now. And another thing's changed. Dad doesn't come round trying to help any more and things run much more smoothly."

"Yes, I've noticed."

"By the way, Neil," she went on, "I thought you might like to have a bigger room when you come back."

He looked at her quickly.

"Come back?"

His mother pushed her sunglasses up into her hair. Her brown eyes were blinking, looking at him anxiously.

"Well, you'll have to come back eventually. We've always known that, haven't we?"

Had they? Neil couldn't remember that ever being said.

"You've had a good break," his mother was saying, "and we've sorted out things here. I think it's time you came back. You'll be able to go back to your school again in September."

"But I like the school where I am," he blurted out. "I really like it. And I like living with Tessa. We leave each other alone."

"Oh." She turned away. "That's all right, then."

He could see how hurt she was and couldn't think how to make it better.

"I mean – sometimes we have blow-ups," he said, "about whose turn it is to wash up or do the ironing or something. But generally we get on all right."

"Well, that's good," she said. She stood up. "Let's go now, shall we?"

"Mum, I –"

She shook her head. "I want you to be happy, Neil. That's all I want."

In the evening he phoned The Hermit Shell.

"Tessa? How's Wayne? Is there any news?"

"There's no change."

"But he's conscious now, isn't he? Sitting up and getting better?"

"Well, no, Neil. He's on a life-support machine. But the

141

whole village is hoping . . ."

He wished he was there with them. He knew people in Portmartin would be stopping each other in the streets to ask about Wayne. There wasn't a person in the village who didn't know him. It was hard to think about things in London while Wayne was hovering between life and death.

3

When Neil and his mother weren't out on their excursions, he sometimes went round to spend time with his father.

They stayed in the flat mostly, watching old movies on TV, playing video games and eating food they fetched from the takeaway. His dad had a girlfriend now, called Sarah, and sometimes she was there too. She seemed quite nice, friendly to Neil and very much at ease with his dad. His dad had lost that hopeful voice he used to put on for Neil in the old days. He was brisker, more matter of fact and, on the whole, that made things easier.

"You seem to have settled down with Tessa very well," he said to Neil one afternoon. "I must say I admire you for that. I didn't think you two would get on. Do you know, I saw an article in a magazine about her pictures the other day. Apparently they're something quite special."

"Yes, they are," said Neil.

His father looked at him.

"I reckon it's done you good, going down there. What does your mother say about it all?"

"She says she wants me to be happy," said Neil.

"Right." His dad touched his shoulder. "That's what I want too, Neil. Just that."

Then he coughed and switched over to another TV channel and no more was said.

Things with his father were certainly better than they'd once been. Perhaps the two of them were beginning to find a space between them that felt right. Neil couldn't stop to work it all out at present. Just at the moment he had other things to think about.

"Tessa? Tell me about Wayne. Is he any better?"

"I'm sorry, Neil, there's no change."

4

Now and again he would bump into Miss Cobham in the corridors. On his last day he stopped to talk to her as she got out of the lift on her way back upstairs from lunch. As usual, she had a book tucked into her pocket that she'd been reading during the meal.

"I've got to take my mind off everyone wittering on and chewing. And all those *dentures*." She rolled up her eyes and shuddered. "Eating's so incredibly boring, Neil. How many years of my life have I spent doing it?"

But she seemed quite cheerful. Her legs were a little better and she told Neil an old friend had left her some money. She said she was thinking of giving herself a little holiday.

They started to walk slowly towards her room. She

looked at him with her bright eyes. He was as tall as she was now.

'So you found your hermit shell," she said.

"I had to go," he said. "I just had to."

"Oh, quite." She nodded. "I could see that at the time. It was a tough thing to do, though, Neil. I used to find her crying, you know."

"Who?"

"Your mother. After you went. In the office, in the linen cupboard . . . all over the place."

He was startled. "Why?"

"Because she felt she'd failed as a mother, I expect," said Miss Cobham. "And she missed you. She missed you and she still does. Both your parents do."

"I know," said Neil, "but –"

The phone by Miss Cobham's room had been ringing for some minutes.

"Dratted thing," said Miss Cobham. As they came level with it, she snatched it up.

"This is the Quiet Corner Rest Home. You are speaking to Miss Primrose Cob – Ah. Yes. Yes, he's here with me as it happens. For you, Neil."

She handed him the phone, smiled at him, and went into her room.

"Neil."

"Yes?"

It was Tessa. She was talking very slowly and carefully, as if she thought he wouldn't be able to follow what she was saying. It was about being sorry, about there being no easy way to tell him this, about them all thinking he should know as soon as possible, that he would want to know before he came back.

He knew of course. But his mind didn't want to take it in.

Then at last the words she was saying dropped into place and his stomach turned over, for what she was finding it so hard to say was that Wayne had died that morning.

CHAPTER TEN

Roses and Bunting

The big silver car came swooping down the motorway next morning. At Exeter it switched from the M5 to the A38 and by one o'clock it was through Plymouth and crossing the Tamar into Cornwall. By the middle of the afternoon it had passed St Austell and Truro and was cresting the last hill.

Looking out, Neil saw the roofs of Portmartin and, beyond that, the blue sea.

Miss Cobham leaned over and patted his hand. "It will be all right, Neil."

He nodded.

"Really all right."

Neil wished he was so sure. Ever since Tessa's phone

call yesterday he'd felt dazed, his mind in turmoil. Even as he told the news about Wayne first to Miss Cobham, and then to his mother, there had only been one clear thought in his mind. He must get back to Portmartin as quickly as he could.

"Why not stay on here for an extra day or two?" his mother had said. "Things are bound to be upsetting in Cornwall. Stay here till they settle down."

But he wanted to go back. He dreaded it but, at the same time, he thought it was where he belonged.

He'd never expected to travel in such style, though. He'd been all prepared to go back on the train as usual.

"I have an idea," announced Miss Cobham.

"What?"

She'd smiled. "We could go together," she said.

It was like Miss Cobham to make rapid decisions, he thought, and to make them seem so simple.

She'd already decided to take a holiday. Where better to go than Cornwall, where she'd been so happy in her childhood? And what better time to go than now, seeing that Neil was already going? Not by train, which she didn't think her legs would like, but by car, a nice comfortable hired car with a nice driver. That way, she could take her wheelchair along.

One phone call and it was arranged. And now, here they were, driving down into Portmartin in a chauffeur-driven car.

The driver turned round to the back seat. "Where now?"

"Ship Street, please," Neil said. "Round by the harbour

and up the hill."

The car had to go slowly. The driver found a way through the holiday-makers round the harbour, and the car bumped over the cobbles towards the lifeboat house.

"Oh," cried Neil, "stop, stop."

He sat for a moment, staring. Then he opened the car door and got out.

There were flowers outside the boat house, a glowing heap of colour on the pavement. Big bunches of flowers and little nosegays and three single red roses. There were cards, too. Neil bent down to read them.

'To a very brave young man,' one said. On another card, someone had written: 'We will remember you, Wayne.'

He got back in the car. They drove to The Hermit Shell and there was Tessa coming out to meet them.

2

The next three days passed quietly.

Miss Cobham had settled herself comfortably in a small guest house, where she had a room on the ground floor looking straight out on the harbour. Outside her room was a seat in the sun. From there she could keep her eye on everyone's comings and goings and, she told Neil, really smell the sea.

"You'll want to look round the village," Craig said when he came over to Portmartin and met her for the first time. "You don't want to miss anything. We'll take you round."

"My dear boy, up these streets?" protested Miss

Cobham, but they did it. Neil and Annis and Craig pushed her wheelchair together up the steep hills, hanging on as a brake on the way down. They squeezed her in and out of souvenir shops, they all had ice-creams from a kiosk, and finally they took her onto the beach itself. They carried her, wheelchair and all, across the sand and enthroned her on the edge of the sea.

"Oh, that's right," she said, as they stood panting. She bent down and scooped up some sand. "I've waited a long time for this."

She sat there all afternoon, breathing in the sea air, her face aglow with happiness.

But it was a sad time too, of course.

Neil sat with Tessa one morning in the studio, gazing out on the sea, while she told him about Wayne.

"It was very peaceful at the end, Neil," she said, "very calm."

She explained that Wayne had really died when that mast had struck him. The rest of the time, in hospital, was making very, very sure that there was no possible hope that he could recover. And then all that could be done was to let him go.

Tessa seemed very peaceful and calm, too. Neil relaxed, breathing in the familiar smells of paint and turpentine and the salty air blowing through the open window. He looked out at the quiet sea.

"Isn't that the lifeboat going out?" He screwed up his eyes against the sun.

Tessa nodded. "Mat said they were going out on exercise this morning. They've got a new crew member to settle in, of course."

"Who is it?"

"John Penna, Wayne's brother." She shook her head. "So many Pennas have served in the lifeboat over the years. They all know the dangers, but nothing seems to stop them offering to fill a place."

An idea came to Neil then, just the germ of an idea. One day, when he'd prepared himself properly, there might be a place in the crew of the Portmartin lifeboat for him.

3

The funeral was on Friday afternoon.

The church was packed to the doors, so full that people had to stand in the road outside and listen to the service relayed by loudspeaker.

Neil sat between Tessa and Annis. Annis had been very quiet the past few days, and Neil knew it was because here at last was proof that awful things could happen, and do happen. But she went to the funeral and she kept her head up as the coffin went past them to the front of the church. Neil himself tried not to look, tried not to think about what was inside that plain wooden box with the yellow and white roses on the top.

But then Mat, very pale, but upright and firm as ever, got up and went to the front and read the lesson in a strong voice. It was about those who go down to the sea in ships and do business in great waters, and how the storm will be made calm and the waves still. And at the end of the service they all sang the old lifeboat hymn 'Eternal Father Strong to Save':

> From rock and tempest, fire and foe,
> Protect them wheresoe'er they go.

One day in the café, Wayne had told Neil how once he'd been out in a bad storm, and he had seen waves so massive they scooped up all the water around the boat for a moment. He'd looked down and seen terrible jagged rocks deep on the sea-bed, rocks never normally uncovered or seen.

"Weren't you scared?" Neil had asked.

"You bet I was scared," said Wayne, "but I wouldn't have missed it. You don't see things like that if you sit at home."

Everyone in the church stood still after the hymn ended. Then Mat, John Penna and four other members of the lifeboat crew stepped forward. They took the coffin on their shoulders and bore it out of the church. This time Neil did watch, because now he knew it wasn't really Wayne inside there: it was only his body. The words that Mat had read were still ringing in his ears. Wayne had gone down to the sea, had chosen to go, had helped to save lives and done what was right. He had passed over the rock and the tempest into peace and calm.

The organ played. They came out of the cool church into the sunshine and saw the sea sparkling below them, as serene and quiet as Neil had ever seen it.

Tessa hugged his arm.

"Are you all right, Neil?"

"Yes, I am," he said and hugged her back. He had not expected the funeral would make him feel better, but it had. He was glad he'd had the courage to come back.

4

Before long, it was carnival day.

At first, Neil hadn't been able to see how Portmartin was going to be able to put on a carnival only eight days after Wayne's funeral. For a few days the streets had been quiet and sad, Penna's Café had been closed and everyone had spoken in hushed voices. But –

"Of course we'll have the carnival," Mat had declared. "That's what the Pennas want, that's what Wayne would have wanted, and I think we should make it the biggest and best carnival we've ever had."

Saturday morning dawned still and hot. Neil woke up. There was a voice downstairs in the studio, then he heard Tessa laughing. He got out of bed and padded down the stairs.

"What is it?"

"It's the bunting." Tessa's voice was muffled. She was leaning perilously out of the open window. Neil went nearer and saw Mat across the street, hanging out of his own upstairs window in the house with the yellow shutters.

"Here it comes again," he shouted. "Catch!"

"Help!"

Tessa staggered back as a bundle of multi-coloured

bunting was thrown across the street and landed on their floor.

"Well done. Now tie it on," called Mat. "Chuck the rest of it down to the next house. Hurry, we've got the whole of Ship Street to dress up."

Later that morning Neil went down to the harbour.

"Hang on." Tessa ran down the studio stairs. "I'll come with you."

"Aren't you painting?" Tessa seemed to paint every single day of her life.

"Not today. Wayne's sisters are going to work at thc café. The place is going to be terribly busy with the carnival on and John's in the procession, of course. So I offered to work there today."

"Oh, right," said Neil.

"Let the painting wait for once, that's what I thought."

"Right."

"I'll be in the kitchen, you know, washing dishes, that sort of thing."

"Really?" He raised his eyebrows. "You'rc going to work in a kitchen all day?"

She eyed him.

"Why not? That's enough of that, young man. Just you wait and see."

5

It seemed that every street in Portmartin was criss-crossed with bunting by now. Neil parted from Tessa at Penna's Café. Its door stood wide open, and a big board declared 'CARNIVAL SPECIALS'. Tables and chairs had spilled outside and people sat in the sun drinking coffee.

He spent the rest of the morning making himself useful at the boat house, where there was to be an RNLI stall and guided tours of the station.

"All ready for this afternoon, Annis, Neil?" asked Mat. "The procession?"

"Yes, fine."

He'd rather dreaded the procession. He was to have been with Wayne and now he wouldn't be, but in the end it was all right, it was fun.

For one thing, the parade was led by a brass band that had arrived by coach from town, and it was the band in which Craig played trombone. Neil, who wasn't at all musical himself, envied him his splendid blue and gold uniform and his shining instrument.

"Bloomin' hot work today, mind," said Craig, his broad face already glistening. He went off to line up with the others.

"All ready?" called the bandmaster.

The floats and the marchers jostled into place on the playing field at the top of the village, and a hush fell. Then the signal was given.

Thump. Thump. Thump.

First the big drum alone. Then it was joined by the blare

of brass. The lorries revved up, another band at the back began to play, and they were away, round the field, out into Longview Road and down the slow, winding route to the harbour. All the way down through Portmartin's narrow packed streets, Neil kept his eye on Craig's broad back ahead, saw his red cheeks bulging as he blew, and felt cheered.

After all, who could feel depressed when they were shaking a bucket under people's noses for them to drop money in, and walking alongside a float of large hairy Portmartin fishermen wearing satin dresses and dancing the can-can? In the end, they'd decided not to dress as piskies as Wayne had suggested, and Neil was wearing a pirate's hat and eyepatch.

"For the lifeboat," Neil chanted over and over. "All money to the lifeboat."

He had never felt more a part of Portmartin. Wayne's brother John was walking with him, Annis and Mat were just behind. He knew that to the strangers lining the streets he looked no different from anyone else in the procession. He looked Portmartin born and bred.

They reached the harbour, where the crowds were thickest. He saw Miss Cobham waving from her wheelchair on the edge of the pavement. By then the bucket was as heavy as he could swing.

"Great going, everybody," said Mat, handing over the buckets to someone for counting. "Now off you go and enjoy yourselves."

For the rest of the afternoon, Neil and Annis and Craig did just that. They watched the races between the fishing boats decked with flags and loaded with supporters and crates of beer. They took Miss Cobham on a tour of the stalls round the harbour. Craig won a tin of pineapple on the tombola and Annis won a fluffy monkey on the hoopla. Finally, they went into Penna's Café for some ice-cream.

The café was packed to the doors, and they had to squeeze through to get to the counter.

"I'll go and see if Tessa needs any help," said Neil. He pushed open the kitchen door.

"Oh, sorry –" he said.

"Neil, we were just . . . just . . ."

Tessa, rather pink in the face, her hair in a mess, turned hastily back to the sink. Mat, who had been standing very close to her, grinned at Neil and reached out a hand for a tea-towel.

" . . .just getting these dishes done," said Tessa, throwing a handful of cutlery into the sink. "Weren't we, Mat?"

6

In the evening there were going to be fireworks. Before that, Miss Cobham came to have supper at The Hermit Shell.

She sat with Neil at the kitchen table, drinking a glass of wine.

"It's been another lovely day," she said. Her holiday

was due to end in a couple of days. "There is, truly, nowhere quite like Cornwall. I knew that when I was six and came here for the first time on holiday."

Neil got up to stir the soup. Tessa had started the supper, then slipped upstairs to the studio, murmuring something about coming back in a second or two. She hadn't been seen since.

"So long ago," said Miss Cobham. "I used to stay not very far from here with my mother and father, just along the coast, always the same place. And the first morning, going down to the beach, I'd run ahead. I used to throw myself down by the rock-pools and just lie there, gazing into the water, smelling the seaweed, seeing those little fish darting . . . the crabs scuttling . . . I was very happy."

She smiled up at Neil.

"Do you know, when I was very small, I used to think I could take some of it home with me. One year we were all packed up to catch the train, and Father suddenly said, "What's that you've got there, Primrose?" I showed him my little seaside bucket. It was full of sea creatures sloshing around in water from a rock pool." She sighed. "Of course, he marched me straight down to the beach to put it all back. And I cried. Every year, I tried it again and then I'd cry again."

Her wine glass was empty. Neil pushed the bottle nearer to her and looked in the oven at the cauliflower cheese. It was bubbling nicely. He started to make a salad.

"Then I grew up," went on Miss Cobham, "and I learnt you don't need to carry a rock-pool round with you in order to remember it. And then I wasn't very happy at home so I got the job with the Rangold Line and that was marvellous. I'd always loved the sea so much. Backwards and forwards across the Atlantic I went, round the whole world sometimes. A dream job. And I thought, when I retired, I'd go and live in Cornwall, right by the sea, and make all my dreams come true."

"Like the Rangold poster," said Neil, slicing tomatoes.

"Yes. But perhaps nothing can make *all* your dreams come true. That one never came true for me. I had to give up work to help look after Father. Then Mother was ill for a long, long time. By the time she died, most of the money had gone. And now my legs have too." She laughed and helped herself to a radish to nibble.

"So it was the Quiet Corner Rest Home for me. And your parents have been very kind to me."

She darted one of her quick bird glances at him. He was shredding lettuce at the sink now. "They're good people, Neil. Both of them."

She paused. He didn't say anything.

"And they'd like you back in London. One day soon."

He went on shredding lettuce and didn't turn round.

After a minute, she said, "That morning you left, you talked about being a hermit crab in a shell, cruising round the sea and holding the entrance shut with your claw. Do you remember?"

He turned round. "Yes."

"But even hermit crabs grow," she said. "They put their heads out, they wave a claw or two. Nobody wants to spend their whole life curled up in a shell, holding the door shut. My book says when a hermit crab has been in its shell a long time, it grows right out of the shell and has to go and look for a bigger one. Quite frightening. But I bet it finds one thing."

In the living room, the phone began to ring. He heard Tessa running down to answer it.

"What does it find?" he asked.

"If it has done all this growing," said Miss Cobham, "its old enemies will look quite small. I'll have another radish if you don't mind."

He gave her one. Then he found a bowl and arranged the salad, thinking about what she had said.

He'd had enemies once. He had to think quite hard to recall their names. Martyn and Lee, that was it. He remembered their faces, pressed to the glass as the underground train whirled them away into the tunnel. They were nothing to him now.

There were lots of different ways of living. He could go to school in London, and be in Cornwall for the holidays. Or the other way round. There were lots of different ways of doing things.

"What do you think?" asked Miss Cobham.

"I'll let you know," said Neil.

Tessa came in.

"Sorry." She pushed her hand through her hair, making it even untidier. She saw the salad, saw Neil slicing crusty bread. "Neil, that's brilliant. Sorry. I had this idea for a new painting and I simply had to go up and try it out. Then Mat rang –"

"We could have the soup now," said Neil. "Sit down."

Tessa sat down.

"Guess what happened this afternoon, when we were washing up?" she said. "Mat asked me to marry him."

"That's very nice," said Miss Cobham. "What did you tell him?"

"I said no," said Tessa. "I mean, I like things as they are, painting all day, living in The Hermit Shell. I don't want anything to change. But he's just rung and asked me again. He said Annis is really keen on the idea. He said . . . Oh, all sorts of things . . . and I said –"

"What?"

"I said I'd let him know," said Tessa.

She smiled at them both and picked up her soup spoon. "Let's eat," she said. "And then we'll go and watch the fireworks."